Paul Durcan was bor. ... ... 944, of County Mayo parents, and studied archaeology and medieval history at University College Cork. His first book, *Endsville* (with Brian Lynch), appeared in 1967, and has been followed by 17 others, including *O Westport in the Light of Asia Minor* (1975), *Teresa's Bar* (1976), *Sam's Cross* (1978), *Jesus, Break His Fall* (1980), *The Selected Paul Durcan* (edited by Edna Longley, Poetry Ireland Choice, 1982), *Jumping the Train Tracks with Angela* (1983), *The Berlin Wall Café* (Poetry Book Society Choice, 1985), *Going Home to Russia* (1987), *Daddy, Daddy* (1990), *Crazy about Women* (1991), *Christmas Day* (1996), and *Greetings to Our Friends in Brazil* (1999). In 1974 he won the Patrick Kavanagh Award and in 1978 and 1980 received Creative Writing Bursaries from the Arts Council/An Chomhairle Ealaíon, Ireland. Apart from Britain and Ireland, where he reads regularly, he has read in Yugoslavia, the former Soviet Union, the USA (where in 1985 he was resident poet at The Frost Place, New Hampshire), Canada, Holland (at the Rotterdam International Poetry Festival), France, Italy, Luxembourg, Belgium, New Zealand, Israel, Germany, Brazil, Portugal, Catalonia, Austria, the Czech Republic, and Japan. In October 1989 he received the Irish American Cultural Institute Poetry Award and in 1990 won the Whitbread Poetry Award with *Daddy, Daddy*. In the same year he was Writer in Residence at Trinity College Dublin. He is a member of Aosdána and lives in Dublin.

Paul Durcan

A SNAIL IN MY PRIME

Selected Poems

THE HARVILL PRESS
LONDON

First published in 1993 by Harvill

This edition first published in 1999 by The Harvill Press

11

The Harvill Press
Random House, 20 Vauxhall Bridge Road
London SW1V 2SA

www.randomhouse.co.uk

Addresses for companies within
The Random House Group Limited can be found at:
www.randomhouse.co.uk/offices.htm

The Random House Group Limited Reg. No. 954009

A CIP catalogue record for this book
is available from the British Library

ISBN 9781860461873

Penguin Random House is committed to a sustainable future for
our business, our readers and our planet. This book is made from
Forest Stewardship Council® certified paper.

Printed and bound in Great Britain by Clays Ltd, Elcograf S.p.A.

Photoset in Monotype Bembo by Servis Filmsetting, Manchester

TO SHEILA MACBRIDE DURCAN

Mother most missed, for all
The films, plays, books
You gave, brought me to,
Who when I lost all
Stood by me always,
Take this book, smile,
Go to bed, conclude:
Mud on your shoes, son,
Mud on your shoes.

ACKNOWLEDGEMENTS

With the exception of the poems in "A Snail in My Prime", which ar
published here in book form for the first time, the poems in this selection
are taken from the following collections: *Endsville* (with Brian Lynch),
New Writers Press, Dublin, 1967; *O Westport in the Light of Asia Minor*,
Anna Livia Press, Dublin, 1975; *Teresa's Bar*, Gallery Press, Dublin, 1976,
1986; *Sam's Cross*, Profile Press, Dublin, 1978; *Jesus, Break His Fall* (Raven
Arts Press, Dublin, 1980); *The Selected Paul Durcan*, edited by Edna
Longley, Blackstaff Press, Belfast, 1982; *Jumping the Train Tracks with
Angela*, Raven Arts Press, Dublin, 1983 and Carcanet New Press,
Manchester, 1983; *The Berlin Wall Café*, Blackstaff Press, Belfast, 1985;
Going Home to Russia, Blackstaff Press, Belfast, 1987; *Jesus and Angela*,
Blackstaff Press, Belfast, 1988; *Daddy, Daddy*, Blackstaff Press, Belfast,
1990; *Crazy about Women*, National Gallery of Ireland, Dublin, 1991.

CONTENTS

I would like my pictures to look as if a human being had passed between them, like a snail, leaving a trail of the human presence and memory trace of past events as the snail leaves its slime.

FRANCIS BACON

The White Window

Of my love's body I think
That it is a white window.
Her clothes are curtains:
By day drawn over
To conceal the light;
By night drawn back
To reveal the dark.

Nessa

I met her on the First of August
In the Shangri-La Hotel,
She took me by the index finger
And dropped me in her well.
And that was a whirlpool, that was a whirlpool,
And I very nearly drowned.

Take off your pants, she said to me,
And I very nearly didn't;
Would you care to swim, she said to me,
And I hopped into the Irish Sea.
And that was a whirlpool, that was a whirlpool,
And I very nearly drowned.

On the way back I fell in the field
And she fell down beside me,
I'd have lain in the grass with her all my life
With Nessa:
She was a whirlpool, she was a whirlpool,
And I very nearly drowned.

O Nessa my dear, Nessa my dear,
Will you stay with me on the rocks?
Will you come for me into the Irish Sea
And for me let your red hair down?
And then we will ride into Dublin City
In a taxi-cab wrapped up in dust.
Oh you are a whirlpool, you are a whirlpool,
And I am very nearly drowned.

November 30, 1967

to Katherine

I awoke with a pain in my head
And my mother standing at the end of the bed;
"There's bad news in the paper," she said,
"Patrick Kavanagh is dead."

After a week which was not real
At last I settled down to a natural meal;
I was sitting over a pint and a beef sandwich
In Mooney's across the street from the Rotunda.

By accident I happened to tune in
To the conversation at the table from me;
I heard an old Northsider tell to his missus
"He was pure straight, God rest him, not like us."

The Girl with the Keys to Pearse's Cottage

to John and Judith Meagher

When I was sixteen I met a dark girl;
Her dark hair was darker because her smile was so bright;
She was the girl with the keys to Pearse's Cottage;
And her name was Cáit Killann.

The cottage was built into the side of a hill;
I recall two windows and cosmic peace
Of bare brown rooms and on whitewashed walls
Photographs of the passionate and pale Pearse.

I recall wet thatch and peeling jambs
And how all was best seen from below in the field;
I used sit in the rushes with ledger-book and pencil
Compiling poems of passion for Cáit Killann.

Often she used linger on the sill of a window;
Hands by her side and brown legs akimbo;
In sun-red skirt and moon-black blazer;
Looking toward our strange world wide-eyed.

Our world was strange because it had no future;
She was America-bound at summer's end.
She had no choice but to leave her home –
The girl with the keys to Pearse's Cottage.

O Cáit Killann, O Cáit Killann,
You have gone with your keys from your own native place.
Yet here in this dark – El Greco eyes blaze back
From your Connemara postman's daughter's proudly mortal
    face.

4

O Westport in the Light of Asia Minor

I

Feet crossed, arms behind his head,
God lay below the skyline hidden from sight;
And Gauloise smoke trailed up the sky.

British frocks and dresses lay draped on the rocks,
Grey flashing windows of a nineteenth-century boutique,
While on the sands the girls lay lazily on their sides
All moon in the daylight
Musing "What is he like?" but at the back of their minds
The heart raged on:
Flame seamed with all the scorn of a soldier
Saying "After the battle".

II

But often the Reek would stand with a cloud round its head;
Behind the sky stood God with a cleaver raised;
Yet when cocky men peered round the curtain of sky
There was no god and the mists came,
Lay down on the west coast,
Fur off the back of a graveyard,
As if an ape had got the tedium of a thousand years between his
    maulers
And shoved it across the world onto our land:
The mists put the fear of our mother into us:
I am what I am for fear of hiding in the action
And yet —

If this world is not simply atmosphere pierced through and
    through
With the good doubt,
Then here it was Red Riding Hood who was laid up in bed;
It was Red-Eared Black Tongue who crouched at the bedside;
And she did the child no harm but good.

But there were some who had guts, took action and stayed;
And standing on the mountains of their dread saw
The islands come up through the mists—
Seductive garments that a man would dream of—
And with the islands finally the sun;
Black at the edges, pure red at the centre.

They came at a run down the mountain
Landing with such falls that even the few small hard gold pieces
    in their pockets
Smashed into pieces so infinitesimal that not even a Shylock
    ever would find them;
They came starting out of their breeches out onto the stony
    shore,
The sea was a great unnamed flower whose leaves they stood
    under
And danced to ring upon ring;
Thin prickly bearded men casting ridiculousness to the
    multitude,
Casting it in great armfuls made bountiful by the slow and
    graceful whirling of their arms,
And they sang: As though a rock were naked.

They Say the Butterfly Is
the Hardest Stroke

to Richard Riordan

From coves below the cliffs of the years
I have dipped into *Ulysses,*
A Vagrant, Tarry Flynn –
But for no more than ten minutes or a page;
For no more than to keep in touch
With minds kindred in their romance with silence.
I have not "met" God, I have not "read"
David Gascoyne, James Joyce, or Patrick Kavanagh:
I believe in them.
Of the song of him with the world in his care
I am content to know the air.

Combe Florey

to Laura Waugh

Wilderness that not always would deliver:
But to us come from the hot clink of London
It was Tel Aviv, the Hill of Spring and Garden of the Sea
To wake in the mornings and to hear the stillness —
And that in spite or because of
The racket of birds — more than one
Woodpecker inhabited the oak outside my window
And at six each morning wound up their clocks in a loud
    manner
Not to speak of the woodpigeon, the cuckoo, the others
Whose names I do not know.
I said to the woman of the house in my own painful and
    boulder fashion:
It is a crying shame to be a creature of this earth
And not know the names of the birds in the trees
And yet I know the names of fifty motor cars.
She said: Lord, I do not think I know the name of even one of
    the little creatures.
And so saying, she gave tiny feet back to my boulder and pain.

La Terre des Hommes

Fancy meeting *you* out here in the desert:
Hallo Clockface.

Aughawall Graveyard

Lonely lonely lonely lonely:
The story with a middle only.

Ireland 1972

Next to the fresh grave of my beloved grandmother
The grave of my first love murdered by my brother.

The Night They Murdered
Boyle Somerville

As I was travelling one morning in an empty carriage
On a train passing south through the west
A small old woman with her husband who was smaller
Hobbled in, shut the door and sat down.
They told me they were going home to Skibbereen,
That they were old-age pensioners and proud of it
Enjoying free travel up and down the country.
They sat down opposite me and we conversed
When it suited us
Such was the ease with which we comported our silences.
Outside, the fields in their summer, lay on their sides in the sun,
Their season of flashing over.
Nor did we evade each other's eyes
Nor pronounce solutions to the awful war-in-progress
Except by a sign-language acknowledging
That here was the scar that lay *inside* the wound,
The self-betrayal beyond all chat.
And all this ease and all this sombre wisdom came
Not from me who am not by nature wise
But from the two old-age pensioners in their seventies.
He was a king-figure from out the islands of time,
A short round-shouldered man with a globe of a skull
Whose lips were the lips of an African chieftain
Having that expression from which there is no escape,
A gaze of the lips,
Interrupted only by the ritual blowing of an ancient pipe.
His wife – being a queen – told him to put away his pipe;
Did he not see the sticker on the windowpane?
It said "Ná Caith Tobac" – but he did not hear her

No more than he heard the ticket inspector
Who having failed to draw attention to the warning notice
Withdrew apologetically, apologising for the intrusion.
So, while the old man blew on his walnut plug
His wife gazed out the window and so did I.
When she spoke, she spoke of the old times and the *scoraíocht*
Back in Skibbereen and of the new times and the new words.
"Ah but," he interposed, glaring out into the blue-walled sky,
"I found out what was in it, and was not in it,
The night they murdered Boyle Somerville;
I knew then that it was only the sky had a roof."
Whereupon beads of sweat trembled on his upper lip
Between the black bristles of his pouring flesh.
Here was an old man, fit to humble death.

1972

The Kilfenora Teaboy

I'm the Kilfenora teaboy
And I'm not so very young,
But though the land is going to pieces
I will not take up the gun;
I am happy making tea,
I make lots of it when I can,
And when I can't—I just make do;
And I do a small bit of sheepfarming on the side.

Oh but it's the small bit of furze between two towns
Is what makes the Kilfenora teaboy really run.

I have nine healthy daughters
And please God I will have more,
Sometimes my dear wife beats me
But on the whole she's a gentle soul;
When I'm not making her some tea
I sit out and watch them all
Ring-a-rosying in the street;
And I do a small bit of sheepfarming on the side.

Oh but it's the small bit of furze between two towns
Is what makes the Kilfenora teaboy really run.

Oh indeed my wife is handsome,
She has a fire lighting in each eye,
You can pluck laughter from her elbows
And from her knees pour money's tears;
I make all my tea for her,

I'm her teaboy on the hill,
And I also thatch her roof;
And I do a small bit of sheepfarming on the side.

Oh but it's the small bit of furze between two towns
Is what makes the Kilfenora teaboy really run.

And I'm not only a famous teaboy,
I'm a famous caveman too;
I paint pictures by the hundred
But you can't sell walls;
Although the people praise my pictures
As well as my turf-perfumèd blend
They rarely fling a fiver in my face;
Oh don't we do an awful lot of dying on the side?

But oh it's the small bit of furze between two towns
Is what makes the Kilfenora teaboy really run.

She Mends an Ancient Wireless

You never claimed to be someone special;
Sometimes you said you had no special talent;
Yet I have seen you rear two dancing daughters
With care and patience and love unstinted;
Reading or telling stories, knitting gansies
And all the while holding down a job
In the teeming city, morning until dusk.
And in the house when anything went wrong
You were the one who fixed it without fuss;
The electricity switch which was neither on nor off,
The TV aerial forever falling out;
And now as I watch you mend an ancient wireless
From my tiny perch I cry once more your praises
And call out your name across the great divide – Nessa.

Teresa's Bar

We sat all day in Teresa's Bar
And talked, or did not talk, the time away;
The only danger was that we might not leave sober
But that is a price you have to pay.
Outside in the rain the powers-that-be
Chemist, draper, garda, priest
Paced up and down in unspeakable rage
That we could sit all day in Teresa's Bar
"Doing nothing".

Behind the bar it was often empty;
Teresa, like all of us,
Besides doing nothing
Had other things to do
Such as cooking meals
Or washing out underwear
For her mad father
And her madder husband,
Or enduring their screams.

But Teresa deep down had no time for time
Or for those whose business has to do with time;
She would lean against the bar and smile through her weariness
By turns being serious and light with us;
Her eyes were birds on the waves of the sea;
A mother-figure but also a sun-girl;
An image of tranquillity but of perpetual creation;
A process in which there is no contradiction
For those with guts not to be blackmailed by time.

There is no time in Teresa's Bar;
The Garda Síochána or the Guardia Civil –
The Junior Chamber or the Roman Curia –
The Poetry Society or the GAA –
The Rugby Club or the Maynooth Hierarchy –
RTE or Conor's Cabaret –
It makes no difference in Teresa's Bar
Where the air is as annotated with the tobacco smoke of
    inventiveness
As the mind of a Berkleyan philosopher.

The small town abounds with rumours
About Teresa's Bar;
A hive of drug-takers (poor bees)
A nest of fornicators (poor birds)
Homosexual not to mention heterosexual;
Poor birds and bees trapped in metaphors of malice.
The truth is that here, as along by the path
By the river that flows along by the edge of the town,
Young and old meet in a life-obtaining sequence
Of days interspersed by nights, seasons by seasons,
Deaths by deaths;
While the members of the resurrection of judgment
Growl and scowl behind arrases in drawing rooms
Here are the members of the resurrection of life
And their tutelary goddess is Teresa
Thirty-five, small, heavy, and dark,
And who would sleep with any man who was honest
    enough
Not to mouth the platitudes of love;
A sensual woman, brave and true,
Bringer of dry wisdom and free laughter
As well as of glasses and bowls,
And who has sent forth into the hostile world

Persons whose universal compassion is infinitesimally more
   catholic
Than that of any scion of academe
Such as James Felix Hennessy
Who has been on the dole for sixteen years
As well as making poems and reading books
And who when accused of obscenity
By the Right Rev. Fr O'Doherty
Riposted with all the humility of Melchisedech:
"You must learn the reality of the flesh, Father;
You must learn the reality of the flesh."

If there be a heaven
Heaven would be
Being with Teresa
Inside the rain;
So let's lock up the bar, Teresa,
Lay ourselves on the floor,
Put some more coal on the fire,
Pour ourselves each a large whiskey;
Let's drink to Teresa of Teresa's Bar
Reclining on the floor with one of her boys,
And big black coals burning bright,
And yellowest whiskey in a brown bottle,
And outside a downpour relentlessly pouring down.

The Hat Factory

Eleven o'clock and the bar is empty
Except for myself and an old man;
We sit with our backs to the street-window,
The sun in the east streaming through it;
And I think of childhood and swimming
Underwater by a famine pier;
The ashlar coursing of the stonework
Like the bar-room shelves
Seen through tidal amber seaweed
In the antique mirror;
Now myself and the old man floating
In the glow of the early morning sun
Twined round each other and our newspapers;
And our pint glasses like capstans on the pier.
We do not read our daily charters —
Charters of liberty to know what's going on —
But hold them as capes before reality's bull
And with grace of ease we make our passes;
El Cordobes might envy this old small man
For the sweet veronicas he makes in daily life.
He is the recipient of an old-age pension
While I am that low in society's scale
I do not rate the dole
But I am at peace with myself and so is he;
Although I do not know what he is thinking
His small round fragile noble mouth
Has the look of the door of Aladdin's cave
Quivering in expectation of the magic words;
Open sesame;

I suspect that like me he is thinking
Of the nothing-in-particular;
Myself, I am thinking of the local hat factory,
Of its history and the eerie fact
That in my small town I have never known
Anyone who worked in it
Or had to do with it at all;
As a child I used look through a hole in the hedge
At the hat factory down below in the valley;
I used lie flat on my face in the long grass
And put out my head through the hole;
Had the hatters looked out through their porthole windows
They would have seen high up in the hillside
A long wild hedgerow broken only
By the head of the child looking out through the hole;
I speculate;
And as to what kind of hats they make;
And do they have a range in black birettas;
And do they have a conveyor belt of toppers;
And do the workers get free hats?
And I recall the Pope's skull-cap
Placed on my head when as a boy-child
In a city hospital I lay near to death
And the black homburg of the red-nosed undertaker
And the balaclavas of assassins
And the pixies of the lost children of the murdered earth
And the multicoloured yamulka of the wandering Jew
And the black kippa of my American friend
In Jerusalem in the snow
And the portly Egyptian's tiny fez
And the tragic Bedouin's kefia in the sands of sun
And the monk's cowl and the nun's wimple
And the funereal mortarboards of airborn puritans
And the megalithic coifs of the pancake women of Brittany

And the sleek fedoras of well-to-do thugs
And sadistic squires' Napoleonic tricorns
And prancing horse-cavalry in their cruel shakos
And the heroic lifeboatman's black sou'wester
And the nicotine-stained wig of the curly-haired barrister
And the black busby used as a handbag by my laughing brother
And the silken turban of the highbrow widow
And foreign legionaries in nullah kepis
And May Day presidiums in astrakhans
And bonnets and boaters and sombreros and stetsons
And stove-pipes and steeples and mantillas and berets
And topis and sunhats and deerstalkers and pill-boxes
And naughty grandmothers in toques
And bishops' mitres and soldiers' helmets;
And in Languedoc and in Aran – cloth caps.
And what if you were a hatter
And you married a hatter
And all your sons and daughters worked as hatters
And you inhabited a hat-house all full of hats:
Hats, hats, hats, hats.
Hats: the apotheosis of an ancient craft;
And I think of all the nationalities of Israel
And of how each always clings to his native hat,
His priceless and moveable roof,
His hat which is the last and first symbol
Of a man's slender foothold on this earth.
Women and girls also work in the factory
But not many of them wear hats;
Some wear scarves, but rarely hats;
Now there'll be no more courting of maidens
In schooner hats on dangerous cliffs;
It seems part of the slavery of liberation
To empty relationships of all courtship
Of which hats were an exciting part.

Probably, I shall never wear a hat:
So thus I ask the old man
If I may look at his trilby —
Old honesty —
And graciously he hands it to me
And with surprise
I note that it was manufactured
In the local hat factory
And I hand it back to him —
A crown to its king —
And like a king he blesses me when he goes,
Wishing me a good day before he starts
His frail progress home along the streets,
Along the lanes and terraces of the hillside,
To his one up and one down.
I turn about and see
Over the windowpane's frosted hemisphere
A small black hat sail slowly past my eyes
Into the unknown ocean of the sun at noon.

Wife Who Smashed Television Gets Jail

"She came home, my Lord, and smashed in the television;
Me and the kids were peaceably watching *Kojak*
When she marched into the living room and declared
That if I didn't turn off the television immediately
She'd put her boot through the screen;
I didn't turn it off, so instead she turned it off –
I remember the moment exactly because Kojak
After shooting a dame with the same name as my wife
Snarled at the corpse – Goodnight, Queen Maeve –
And then she took off her boots and smashed in the television;
I had to bring the kids round to my mother's place;
We got there just before the finish of *Kojak*;
(My mother has a fondness for *Kojak*, my Lord);
When I returned home my wife had deposited
What was left of the television into the dustbin,
Saying – I didn't get married to a television
And I don't see why my kids or anybody else's kids
Should have a television for a father or mother,
We'd be much better off all down in the pub talking
Or playing bar-billiards –
Whereupon she disappeared off back down again to the pub."
Justice O'Brádaigh said wives who preferred bar-billiards to
    family television
Were a threat to the family which was the basic unit of society
As indeed the television itself could be said to be a basic unit of
    the family
And when as in this case wives expressed their preference in
    forms of violence
Jail was the only place for them. Leave to appeal was refused.

Lord Mayo

I had to go and work in officeblocks in Shepherd's Bush
    And I worked such hours that I could not write letters;
I spent my few free hours in The Railway Tavern talking
    With a Carlow-born clerk and two Belfast bricklayers;
But I came back to you, Lord Mayo.

Now you are older and angrier and I am still young and gay
    And what, my lord, are we going to do?
If you were but to smile once as once you used to
    I'd jump into bed with you for ever;
For I came back to you, Lord Mayo.

I'd go live with you in the wilds of Erris
    Rearing children despite bog and rain;
I'd row with you the dark depths of Beltra and of Conn
    If you'd but smile on me;
For I came back to you, Lord Mayo.

The Baker

After a night at the ovens
In the big city bakery
The baker walks home alone:
He stalks through the dawn
Gropingly
Like a man through a plate-glass door
(There have been many such —
Oh many such — years
And nights of it
And it has been so
Hot)
He feels fragile and eerily pure
Like a loaf new out of oven,
All heat through-and-through,
And he does not look sure
That the air is not a plate-glass door;
So gropingly he stalks
In his hobnailed boots
Up the steep terraced street:
Like a tiny giant walking in glue:
Like a human being about to split in two.

Polycarp

Polycarp has quit the priesthood
And he is living back at home;
He wears a smile upon his lips
That blooms from the marrow bone.

It's a smile that flowers and withers
Like fruit upon a tree;
In winter he stands at corners
In the streets all nakedly.

They are waxing pretty angry —
Are Respectability's crew;
It's a crime against all decency
To be one of the very few

Who has had courage like Polycarp
To be his own sweet self;
Not to mind the small town sneers
When they call him a "fucking elf"

Or the do-it-yourself-men boors
Who despise men with feminine souls;
Boors who when they were boys
Spoke of girls as "ruddy holes"

And now who are married and proper
Living up on Respectability Hill
And in their spare time make their own coffins
Which they use first as coffee tables.

But Polycarp polkas the streets
As free and easy as he feels;
Sometimes he walks on his toes,
Sometimes on his heels.

Yet they'll put him upon his knees
In the amphitheatre soon;
But his smile will wear them down
By the blood-light of the moon;

And in summer's golden rains
He'll burst out in fruit all over;
She's here, she's here, she's here;
And it is Polycarp that knows how to love her.

Swags of red apples are his cheeks;
Swags of yellow pears are his eyes;
Foliages of dark green oaks are his torsos;
And in the cambium of his bark juice lies.

Desire under the steeples and spires,
Polycarp's back in town;
Desire under the steeples and spires,
Polycarp's back in town.

What Is a Protestant, Daddy?

Gaiters were sinister
And you dared not
Glance up at the visage;
It was a long lean visage
With a crooked nose
And beaked dry lips
And streaky grey hair
And they used scurry about
In small black cars
(Unlike Catholic bishops
Stately in big cars
Or Pope Pius XII
In his gold-plated Cadillac)
And they'd make dashes for it
Across deserted streets
And disappear quickly
Into vast cathedrals
All silent and aloof,
Forlorn and leafless,
Their belfry louvres
Like dead men's lips,
And whose congregations, if any,
Were all octogenarian
With names like Iris;
More likely
There were no congregations
And these rodent-like clergymen
Were conspirators;
You could see it in their faces;

But as to what the conspiracies
Were about, as children
We were at a loss to know;
Our parents called them "parsons"
Which turned them from being rodents
Into black hooded crows
Evilly flapping their wings
About our virginal souls;
And these "parsons" had wives—
As unimaginable a state of affairs
As it would have been to imagine
A pope in a urinal;
Protestants were Martians
Light years more weird
Than zoological creatures;
But soon they would all go away
For as a species they were dying out,
Soon there would be no more Protestants . . .
Oh Yea, Oh Lord,
I was a proper little Irish Catholic boy
Way back in the 1950s.

Protestant Old Folks' Coach Tour
of the Ring of Kerry

Although it was a summer's day
It rained as though it was winter;
And I pressed my nose against the windowpane,
The zoo-like windowpane of the coach,
And I closed my eyes and dreamed,
Dreamed that I was swimming,
Swimming in the coves of Kerry
With my young man Danny
And no one else about;
Danny, Danny, dripping wet,
Laughing through his teeth;
Blown to bits at Ypres.
Behind my eyes it is sunshine still
Although he has gone; .
And my mother and father pad about the farm
Like ghosts cut out of cardboard;
When they died I too looked ghostly
But I stayed alive although I don't know how;
Dreaming to put the beehives back on their feet,
Waiting for Danny to come home.
And now I'm keeping house for brother Giles
Who stayed at home today to milk the cows;
Myself, I am a great jowled cow untended
And when I die I would like to die alone.

In Memory of Those Murdered in the Dublin Massacre, May 1974

In the grime-ridden sunlight in the downtown Wimpy bar
I think of all the crucial aeons – and of the labels
That freedom fighters stick onto the lost destinies of unborn
    children;
The early morning sunlight carries in the whole street from
    outside;
The whole wide street from outside through the plate-glass
    windows;
Wholly, sparklingly, surgingly, carried in from outside;
And the waitresses cannot help but be happy and gay
As they swipe at the tabletops with their dishcloths –
Such a moment as would provide the heroic freedom fighter
With his perfect meat.
And I think of those heroes – heroes? – heroes.

And as I stand up to walk out –
The aproned old woman who's been sweeping the floor
Has mop stuck in bucket, leaning on it;
And she's trembling all over, like a flower in the breeze.
She'd make a mighty fine explosion now, if you were to blow
    her up;
An explosion of petals, of aeons, and the waitresses too, flying
    breasts and limbs,
For a free Ireland.

Before the Celtic Yoke

What was it like in Ireland before the Celtic yoke—
Before war insinuated its slime into the forests of the folk?

Elizabethan, Norman, Viking, Celt,
Conquistadores all:
Imperialists, racialists, from across the seas,
Merciless whalesback riders
Thrusting their languages down my virgin throat,
And to rape not merely but to garotte
My human voice:
To screw my soul to orthodoxy and break my neck.

But I survive, recall
That these are but Micky-come-latelies
Puritanical, totalitarian, by contrast with my primal tongue:
My vocabularies are boulders cast up on time's beaches;
Masses of sea-rolled stones reared up in mile-high ricks
Along the shores and curving coasts of all my island;
Verbs dripping fresh from geologic epochs;
Scorched, drenched, in metamorphosis, vulcanicity, ice ages.

No Celt
Nor Viking, Norman, Elizabethan,
Could exterminate me—
I am as palpable and inscrutable
As is a mother to her man-child;
If you would contemplate me
You will know the terror that an old man knows
As he shrinks back from the grassy womb of his chirping
    mamma.

In Ireland before the Celtic yoke I was the voice of Seeing
And my island people's Speaking was their Being;
So go now, brother – cast off all cultural shrouds
And speak like me – like the mighty sun through the clouds.

Parents

A child's face is a drowned face:
Her parents stare down at her asleep
Estranged from her by a sea:
She is under the sea
And they are above the sea:
If she looked up she would see them
As if locked out of their own home,
Their mouths open,
Their foreheads furrowed –
Pursed-up orifices of fearful fish –
Their big ears are fins behind glass
And in her sleep she is calling out to them
    Father, Father
    Mother, Mother
But they cannot hear her:
She is inside the sea
And they are outside the sea.
Through the night, stranded, they stare
At the drowned, drowned face of their child.

Going Home to Mayo, Winter, 1949

Leaving behind us the alien, foreign city of Dublin,
My father drove through the night in an old Ford Anglia,
His five-year-old son in the seat beside him,
The rexine seat of red leatherette,
And a yellow moon peered in through the windscreen.
"Daddy, Daddy," I cried, "pass out the moon,"
But no matter how hard he drove he could not pass out the
    moon.
Each town we passed through was another milestone
And their names were magic passwords into eternity:
Kilcock, Kinnegad, Strokestown, Elphin,
Tarmonbarry, Tulsk, Ballaghaderreen, Ballavarry;
Now we were in Mayo and the next stop was Turlough,
The village of Turlough in the heartland of Mayo,
And my father's mother's house, all oil-lamps and women,
And my bedroom over the public bar below,
And in the morning cattle-cries and cock-crows:
Life's seemingly seamless garment gorgeously rent
By their screeches and bellowings. And in the evenings
I walked with my father in the high grass down by the river
Talking with him – an unheard-of thing in the city.

But home was not home and the moon could be no more
    outflanked
Than the daylight nightmare of Dublin City:
Back down along the canal we chugged into the city
And each lock-gate tolled our mutual doom;
And railings and palings and asphalt and traffic lights,
And blocks after blocks of so-called "new" tenements –

Thousands of crosses of loneliness planted
In the narrowing grave of the life of the father;
In the wide, wide cemetery of the boy's childhood.

Backside to the Wind

A fourteen-year-old boy is out rambling alone
By the scimitar shores of Killala Bay
And he is dreaming of a French Ireland,
Backside to the wind.

What kind of village would I now be living in?
French vocabularies intertwined with Gaelic
And Irish women with French fathers,
Backsides to the wind.

The Ballina Road would become the Rue Humbert
And wine would be the staple drink of the people;
A staple diet of potatoes and wine,
Backsides to the wind.

Monsieur Duffy might be the harbourmaster
And Madame Duffy the mother of thirteen
Tiny philosophers to overthrow Maynooth,
Backsides to the wind.

Father Molloy might be a worker-priest
Up to his knees in manure at the cattle-mart;
And dancing and loving on the streets at evening
Backsides to the wind.

Jean Arthur Rimbaud might have grown up here
In a hillside terrace under the round tower;
Would he, like me, have dreamed of an Arabian Dublin,
Backside to the wind?

Garda Ned MacHale might now be a gendarme
Having hysterics at the crossroads;

Excommunicating male motorists, ogling females,
Backside to the wind.

I walk on, facing the village ahead of me,
A small concrete oasis in the wild countryside;
Not the embodiment of the dream of a boy,
Backside to the wind.

Seagulls and crows, priests and nuns,
Perch on the rooftops and steeples,
And their Anglo-American mores asphyxiate me,
Backside to the wind.

Not to mention the Japanese invasion:
Blunt people as solemn as ourselves
And as humourless; money is our God,
Backsides to the wind.

The medieval Franciscan Friary of Moyne
Stands house-high, roofless, by;
Past it rolls a vast asphalt pipe,
Backside to the wind,

Ferrying chemical waste out to sea
From the Asahi synthetic-fibre plant;
Where once monks sang, wage-earners slave,
Backsides to the wind.

Run on, sweet River Moy,
Although I end my song; you are
The scales of a salmon of a boy,
Backside to the wind.

Yet I have no choice but to leave, to leave,
And yet there is nowhere I more yearn to live
Than in my own wild countryside,
Backside to the wind.

                                          1976

37

Fat Molly

I was fostered out to a woman called Fat Molly:
It was in the year 744
On the other side of the forest from the monk-fort at Kells
Where the bird-men were scribing their magnificent comic
The Book of Kells.
I'd say Molly was about thirty when I went to her
And she taught me the art of passionate kissing:
From minuscule kisses to majuscule
On lips, breasts, neck, shoulders, lips,
And the enwrapping of tongue around tongue.
I was about fourteen
And she used make me kiss her for hours non-stop
And I'd sit in her lap with my hands
Around her waist gulping her down
And eating her green apples
That hung in bunches from her thighs
And the clusters of hot grapes between her breasts
Until from the backs of my ears down to my toes
All of me tingled
And in the backs of her eyes I saw that her glass had no bottom;
Nothing in life afterwards ever tasted quite so luscious
As Fat Molly's kisses;
               O spirals of animals,
Interlaces of birds;
Sweet, warm, wet, were the kisses she kissed;
Juicy oranges on a naked platter.
She lived all alone in a crannóg
Which had an underwater zig-zag causeway
And people said – and it was not altogether a fiction –

That only a completely drunk man
Could successfully negotiate Fat Molly's entrance;
Completely drunk, I used stagger home
And fall asleep in the arms of her laughter:
Oh sweet crucifixion, crucified on each other.

Well, that was half a century ago
And now the Vikings are here –
Bloody foreigners –
And there's nothing but blood in the air:
But thank you Fat Molly for a grand education;
Like all great education it was perfectly useless.

Ireland 1977

"I've become so lonely, I could die"—he writes,
The native who is an exile in his native land:
"Do you hear me whispering to you across the Golden Vale?
Do you hear me bawling to you across the hearthrug?"

Making Love outside Áras an Uachtaráin

When I was a boy, myself and my girl
Used bicycle up to the Phoenix Park;
Outside the gates we used lie in the grass
Making love outside Áras an Uachtaráin.

Often I wondered what de Valera would have thought
Inside in his ivory tower
If he knew that we were in his green, green grass
Making love outside Áras an Uachtaráin.

Because the odd thing was – oh how odd it was –
We both revered Irish patriots
And we dreamed our dreams of a green, green flag
Making love outside Áras an Uachtaráin.

But even had our names been Diarmaid and Gráinne
We doubted de Valera's approval
For a poet's son and a judge's daughter
Making love outside Áras an Uachtaráin.

I see him now in the heat-haze of the day
Blindly stalking us down;
And, levelling an ancient rifle, he says "Stop
Making love outside Áras an Uachtaráin."

Sister Agnes Writes to Her Beloved Mother

Dear Mother, Thank you for the egg cosy;
Sister Alberta (from near Clonakilty)
Said it was the nicest, positively the nicest,
Egg cosy she had ever seen. Here
The big news is that Rev. Mother is pregnant;
The whole convent is simply delighted;
We don't know who the lucky father is
But we have a shrewd idea who it might be:
Do you remember that Retreat Director
I wrote to you about? – The lovely old Jesuit
With a rosy nose – We think it was he –
So shy and retiring, just the type;
Fr P.J. Pegasus SJ.
Of course, it's all hush-hush,
Nobody is supposed to know anything
In case the Bishop – that young hypocrite –
Might get to hear about it.
When her time comes Rev. Mother officially
Will go away on retreat
And the cherub will be reared in another convent.
But, considering the general decline in vocations,
We are all pleased as pea-shooters
That God has blessed the Order of the Little Tree
With another new sapling, all of our own making,
And of Jesuit pedigree, too.
Nevertheless – not a word.
Myself, I am crocheting a cradle shawl;
Hope you're doing your novenas. Love, Aggie.

Irish Hierarchy Bans Colour Photography

After a spring meeting in their nineteenth-century fastness at
    Maynooth
The Irish Hierarchy has issued a total ban on the practice of
    colour photography:
A spokesman added that while in accordance with tradition
No logical explanation would be provided
There were a number of illogical explanations which he would
    discuss;
He stated that it was not true that the ban was the result
Of the Hierarchy's tacit endorsement of racial discrimination;
(And, here, the spokesman, Fr Marksman, smiled to himself
But when asked to elaborate on his smile, he would not
    elaborate
Except to growl some categorical expletives which included the
    word "liberal")
He stated that if the press corps would countenance an unhappy
    pun
He would say that negative thinking lay at the root of the
    ban;
Colour pictures produced in the minds of people,
Especially in the minds (if any) of young people,
A serious distortion of reality;
Colour pictures showed reality to be rich and various
Whereas reality in point of fact was the opposite;
The innate black-and-white nature of reality would have to be
    safeguarded
At all costs and, talking of costs, said Fr Marksman,
It ought to be borne in mind, as indeed the Hierarchy had
    borne in its collective mind,

That colour photography was far costlier than black-and-white
  photography
And, as a consequence, more immoral;
The Hierarchy, stated Fr Marksman, was once again smiting
  two birds with one boulder;
And the joint hegemony of Morality and Economics was being
  upheld.

The total ban came as a total surprise to the accumulated press
  corps
And Irish Roman Catholic pressmen and presswomen present
Had to be helped away as they wept copiously in their cups:
"No more oranges and lemons in Maynooth," sobbed one
  camera boy.
The general public, however, is expected to pay no heed to the
  ban;
Only politicians and time-servers are likely to pay the required
  lip service;
But the operative noun is lip: there will be no hand or foot
  service.
And next year Ireland is expected to become
The EEC's largest moneyspender in colour photography.

This is Claudia Conway, RTE News (Colour), Maynooth.

In Memory: The Miami Showband –
Massacred 31 July 1975

Beautiful are the feet of them that preach the gospel of peace,
Of them that bring glad tidings of good things

In a public house, darkly lit, a patriotic (sic)
Versifier whines into my face: "You must take one side
Or the other, or you're but a fucking romantic."
His eyes glitter hate and vanity, porter and whiskey,
And I realise that he is blind to the braille connection
Between a music and a music-maker.
"You must take one side or the other
Or you're but a fucking romantic":
The whine is icy
And his eyes hang loose like sheets from poles
On a bare wet hillside in winter
And his mouth gapes like a cave in ice;
It is a whine in the crotch of whose fear
Is fondled a dream gun blood-smeared;
It is in war – not poetry or music –
That men find their niche, their glory hole;
Like most of his fellows
He will abide no contradiction in the mind.
He whines: "If there is birth, there cannot be death"
And – jabbing a hysterical forefinger into my nose and eyes –
"If there is death, there cannot be birth."
Peace to the souls of those who unlike my fellow poet
Were true to their trade
Despite death-dealing blackmail by racists:
You made music, and that was all: You were realists
And beautiful were your feet.

Memoirs of a Fallen Blackbird

They liked me when I was on the wing
And I could whistle and I could sing;
But now that I am in my bed of clay
They come no more to be with me.

It was on the main road half way between
Newcastle West and Abbeyfeale;
A juggernaut glanced me as it passed me by
And that was the end of the road for me.

Later that day, as I lay on the verge,
A thin rake of a young man picked me up
Into his trembling hands, and he stared
At me full quarter of an hour, he stared

At me and then he laid me down
And with his hands scooped me a shallow grave;
His soul passed into me as he covered me o'er;
I fear for him now where'er he be.

They liked me when I was on the wing
And I could whistle and I could sing;
But now that I am in my bed of clay
They come no more to be with me.

Micheál Mac Liammóir

"Dear Boy, What a superlative day for a funeral:
It seems St Stephen's Green put on the appareil
Of early springtime especially for me.
That is no vanity: but – dare I say it – humility
In the fell face of those nay-neighers who say we die
At dying-time. Die? Why, I must needs cry
No, no, no, no,
Now I am living whereas before – no –
'Twas but breathing, choking, croaking, singing,
Superb sometimes but nevertheless but breathing:
You should have seen the scene in University Church:
Packed to the hammer-beams with me left in the lurch
All on my ownio up-front centrestage;
People of every nationality in Ireland and of every age;
Old age and youth – Oh, everpresent, oldest, wished-for youth;
And old Dublin ladies telling their beads for old me; forsooth.
'Twould have fired the cockles of John Henry's heart
And his mussels too: only Sarah Bernhardt
Was missing but I was so glad to see Marie Conmee
Fresh, as always, as the morning sea.
We paid a last farewell to dear Harcourt Terrace,
Dear old, bedraggled, doomed Harcourt Terrace
Where I enjoyed, amongst the crocuses, a Continual Glimpse of
    Heaven
By having, for a living partner, Hilton.
Around the corner the canal waters from Athy gleamed
Engaged in their neverending courtship of Ringsend.
Then onward to the Gate – and to the rose-cheeked ghost of
    Lord Edward Longford;

I could not bear to look at Patrick Bedford.
Oh tears there were, there and everywhere,
But especially there; there outside the Gate where
For fifty years we wooed the goddess of our art;
How many, many nights she pierced my heart.
Ach, níl aon tinteán mar do thinteán féin:
The Gate and the *Taibhdhearc* – each was our name;
I dreamed a dream of Jean Cocteau
Leaning against a wall in Killnamoe;
And so I voyaged through all the nations of Ireland with
   McMaster
And played in Cinderella an ugly, but oh so ugly, sister.
Ah but we could not tarry forever outside the Gate;
Life, as always, must go on or we'd be late
For my rendezvous with my brave gravediggers
Who were as shy but snappy as my best of dressers.
We sped past the vast suburb of Clontarf – all those lives
Full of hardworking Brian Borús with their busy wives.
In St Fintan's Cemetery there was spray from the sea
As well as from the noonday sun, and clay on me:
And a green carnation on my lonely oaken coffin.
Lonely in heaven? Yes, I must not soften
The deep pain I feel at even a momentary separation
From my dear, sweet friends. A green carnation
For you all, dear boy. If you must weep, ba(w)ll;
Slán agus Beannacht, Micheál."

March 1978

Lament for Cearbhall Ó Dálaigh

Into a simple grave six feet deep,
Next grave to a Kerry sheepfarmer,
Your plain oak coffin was laid
In a hail of hail:
The gods in the Macgillycuddy's Reeks
(Snow on their summits)
Were in a white, dancing rage
Together with the two don-
Keys who would not budge
From the graveyard,
And the poets and the painters,
The actors and the actresses,
The etchers and the sculptors,
The child-singers — those multiplying few
Who, despite the ever-darkening night,
Believe with their hearts' might
As did you
In a spoken music of the utter earth:

You who, for a brief hour,
Were Chieftain of a Rising People;
Who brought back into Tara's Halls
The blind poets and the blinder harpists;
Who, the brief hour barely ended,
Were insulted massively,
Betrayed
By a sanctimonious bourgeoisie;
And, worse by far,
By *la trahaison des clercs*;

Where were those talented men
In the government of the talents
When the jackbooted
Bourgeois crackled the whip?
The talented men kept their silence,
Their souls committed to finance;
Now hear their mouth-traps snap shut:
"No comment, no comment, no comment, no comment."
Ah, Cearbhall, but in your death
You led them all a merry dance:
Hauling them all out of their soft Dublin haunts,
Out of their Slickness and Glickness,
Out of their Snugvilles and Smugtowns,
You had them travel all the long,
Long way down to Sneem:
Sneem of the Beautiful Knot:
By God, and by Dana,
Cearbhall, forgive me
But it was a joy to watch them
With their wind-flayed faces
Getting all knotted up
In the knot of your funeral;
Wind, rain, hail and sleet,
Were on your side;
And spears of sunlight
Who, like yourself, did not lie;
Blue Lightning,
Gold Thunder.

In all our memories, Cearbhall,
You will remain as fresh
As the green rock jutting up
In mid-stream

Where fresh and salt waters meet
Under the bridge at Sneem.

How the respectability squirmed
In the church when beside your coffin
The Ó Riada choir sang pagan laments
For their dead chieftain:
"O he is my hero, my brave loved one."
Papal Nuncio, bishops, monsignori,
Passed wind in their misericords,
Their stony faces expressionless.
A Gaelic Chinaman whose birthplace
At 85 Main Street, Bray,
Is today a Chinese restaurant
(The Jasmine, owned by Chi Leung Nam);
O tan-man smiling on the mountain,
You are gone from us now, O Yellow Sun:
Small laughing man,
Cearbhall of the merry eyes,
A Gaelic Charlie Chaplin who became
Chief Justice and President,
Hear our mute confessions now:
We were afraid of the man that licks
Life with such relish;
We were not up to your tricks,
Did not deserve you, Cearbhall
Of the City Centre and the Mountain Pool:
Príomh Breitheamh, Uachtarán: Slán.

March 1978

That Propeller I Left in Bilbao

Would you like a whiskey? Good.
That's my girl: how I do like to see
You with a glass of whiskey in your hand,
And that gleam of a smile beneath your hat:

And that gleam of a smile beneath your hat:
But that propeller I left in Bilbao –
I ought to tell you about it now –
But blast it, I won't: let's have a row:

Ow: ow: ow: let's have a row:
Let's pink the pink floor pinker than pink:
I am a pink place in which a pink pig plashes:
You are a pink peach in which a pink babe perishes –

Perishes to be born! Put in a new cassette!
And let the cherry blossom blossom till it fall
Asunder – O my Pink Thunder – asunder
And that propeller I left in Bilbao

Is still that propeller I left in Bilbao:
But you have sheared off all your robes
And you would like, if it pleases me, a second whiskey:
Why of course, my Big Pink Thunderbird –

My Big Pink Thunderbird – why of course –
Do you know how many telephone calls I had today?
The flaming phone never stopped flaming ringing
And all about that propeller I left in Bilbao:

All about that propeller I left in Bilbao:
I said: "Telex" to them all: "Telex":
And now to you, love, Telex For Ever and For Ever Telex,
And may that propeller I left in Bilbao,

Well—may that propeller I left in Bilbao—
That propeller I left in Bilbao—
Propeller I left in Bilbao—
I left in Bilbao.

The Drimoleague Blues

to Sarah and Síabhra

Oh I know this mean town is not always mean
And I know that you do not always mean what you mean
And the meaning of meaning can both mean and not mean:
But I mean to say, I mean to say,
I've got the Drimoleague Blues, I've got the Drimoleague Blues,
I've got the Drimoleague Blues so bad I can't move:
Even if you were to plug in Drimoleague to every oil well in
    Arabia –
I'd still have the Drimoleague Blues.

Oh this town is so mean that it's got its own mean
And that's to be as mean as green, as mean as green:
Shoot a girl dead and win yourself a bride,
Shoot a horse dead and win yourself a car.
Oh I've got the Drimoleague Blues, I've got the Drimoleague Blues,
I've got the Drimoleague Blues so bad I can't move:
Even if you were to plug in Drimoleague to every oil well in
    Arabia –
I'd still have the Drimoleague Blues.

And so on right down to the end of the line
Mean with Mean will always rhyme
And Man with Man: Oh where is the Woman
With the Plough, where is her Daughter with the Stars?
Oh I've got the Drimoleague Blues, I've got the Drimoleague Blues,
I've got the Drimoleague Blues so bad I can't move:
Even if you were to plug in Drimoleague to every oil well in
    Arabia –
I'd still have the Drimoleague Blues.

Sally

Sally, I was happy with *you*.

Yet a dirty cafeteria in a railway station —
In the hour before dawn over a formica table
Confettied with cigarette ash and coffee stains —
Was all we ever knew of a home together.

"Give me a child and let me go":
"Give me a child and let me stay":
She to him and he to her:
Which said *which* and *who* was *who?*

Sally, I was happy with *you*.

The Daughter Finds Her Father Dead

to A. D.

The day that Father died
I went up to wake him at 8.30 a.m.
Before I left home for school:
The night before he had said
Before I went up to bed:
"Remember to wake me at 8.30 a.m.
Remember to wake me at 8.30 a.m."

The day that Father died
At 8.30 a.m. I went up to wake him
And I thought at first he was dead:
He did not move when I shook him,
But then he said, then he said:
"Rider Haggard, Rider Haggard:
Storm Jameson, Storm Jameson."

The day that Father died
Those were the last words he said:
"Rider Haggard, Rider Haggard:
Storm Jameson, Storm Jameson."
I thought then he was alive
But he was dead, he was dead;
When I came home from school he was dead.

The day that Father died
I glimpsed him telescopically:
Inside in his eyes inside in his head
A small voice in a faraway world
Spinning like a tiny coin:

"Rider Haggard, Rider Haggard:
Storm Jameson, Storm Jameson."

Apparently—I suppose I should say
"It seems"—Father was a man
Who thought God was a woman
And that was why he was always sad,
Bad at being glad:
"Rider Haggard, Rider Haggard:
Storm Jameson, Storm Jameson."

He cries and he cries, over and over,
In the empty nights that are emptier
And the dark days that are darker:
"Rider Haggard, Rider Haggard:
Storm Jameson, Storm Jameson":
And I take a look out from my bunk bed
As if all the world were a black silhouette

Or an infinite series of black silhouettes
Brokenly riding the white skyline:
"Rider Haggard, Rider Haggard:
Storm Jameson, Storm Jameson":
And just as my father thought God was a woman,
I think God is a man: are both of us wrong?
Oh if only a horse could write a song:

Oh if only a horse could write a song.

Charlie's Mother

Brendan, does *your* mother have a hold over *you*?
Mine does over *me*. I keep beseeching her
To take her purple-veined hand out of my head
But do you know what she says, the old cabbage?
Stirring and churning her hand round inside in my head
She crows: "Charlie m'boy, you've got a lot of neck."

Mind you, when I think about it, she has a point:
My neck *is* thick and there *is* rather a lot of it;
And look at all the *mun* I have made
Without having to do a flick of work for it.
I rub my neck wryly when Mother crows:
"That's m'boy, Charlie, lots of *mun* for *mum*."

And you know, Brendan – would you like another drink?
Double brandy there, please – I often think, Brendan,
When I look at myself in the mirror each morning –
And I must admit that that's my favourite moment of each
    day –
Even on black bloody days like today – I always see
Somewhere behind my fat neck my tiny little mother winking
    up at me.

Another drink? Certainly Brendan. Double brandy there,
    please.
Down, Bismarck, down. Down, Bismarck, down.
Damned Alsatian bitch but a friendly bitch at heart;
Mother gave her to me as a Christian – I mean
    Christmas – present.

Another drink? Certainly Brendan, quadruple brandy there,
  please.
Down, Bismarck, down. Down, Bismarck, down.

But Brendan, you were saying about Micky Finn of
  Castlepollard
That his mother has run away and left him for another man?
Another case, I'm afraid, of not keeping the hand in the till;
Not enough neck at all at all. Can you hear me, Brendan?
Come on, *a mhic*, straighten up for Christ's sake – or at least for
  Ireland's sake.
Down, Bismarck, down. Down, Bismarck, down.

Brendan, do you realise, you pixillated, feckless sot,
That if my mother came in here just now, as she might very
  well do.
(Mothers tend to eavesdrop in the footsteps of their favourite
  offspring),
She might think that I am to blame for the condition you're in?
You're not just drunk – you're in a coma:
She might even decide to turn Bismarck against me.

Eat him, Bismarck, eat him.
  Eat him, Bismarck, eat him.

Nyum: nyum, nyum, nyum, nyum, nyum; *nyum.*

En Famille, 1979

Bring me back to the dark school – to the dark school of
   childhood:
To where tiny is tiny, and massive is massive.

Madman

Every child has a madman on their street:
The only trouble about *our* madman is that he's our father.

This Week the Court Is Sleeping
in Loughrea

The perplexed defendants stand upright in the dock
While round about their spiked and barred forecastle,
Like corpses of mutinous sailors strewn about the deck
Of a ghost schooner becalmed in summer heat,
Recline solicitors in suits and barristers in wigs and gowns,
Snoring in their sleeves.
On high, upon the judge's bench,
His Lordship also snores,
Dreaming of the good old days as a drunken devil
Dozing in Doneraile.
From a hook in the ceiling the Court Crier hangs,
His eyes dangling out of their sockets.
Below him the Registrar is smoothing the breasts of his
    spectacles.
In the varnished witness box crouches Reverend Father Perjury
With a knife through his back.
Behind him in the dark aisles, like coshed dummies, lurk
Policemen stupefied by *poitín*.
Up in the amphitheatre of the public gallery
An invisible mob are chewing the cud.
An open window lets in the thudding sounds of blows
As, on the green, tinker men brawl,
As they have done so there down the centuries –
The Sweeneys and the Maughans.
Such slender justice as may be said to subsist in Loughrea
Is to be discerned
In the form of a streamlet behind the house-backs of the town,
Which carries water out to the parched fields
Where cleg-ridden cattle wait thirsty in the shadowy lees,

Their domain far away from the sleeping courtroom of human
  battle.
Is it any surprise that there are children who would rather be
  cattle?

Tullynoe: Tête-à-Tête in the Parish Priest's Parlour

"Ah, he was a grand man."

"He was: he fell out of the train going to Sligo."

"He did: he thought he was going to the lavatory."

"He did: in fact he stepped out the rear door of the train."

"He did: God, he must have got an awful fright."

"He did: he saw that it wasn't the lavatory at all."

"He did: he saw that it was the railway tracks going away from him."

"He did: I wonder if . . . but he was a grand man."

"He was: he had the most expensive Toyota you can buy."

"He had: well, it was only beautiful."

"It was: he used to have an Audi."

"He had: as a matter of fact he used to have two Audis."

"He had: and then he had an Avenger."

"He had: and then he had a Volvo."

"He had: in the beginning he had a lot of Volkses."

"He had: he was a great man for the Volkses."

"He was: did he once have an Escort?"

"He had not: he had a son a doctor."

"He had: and he had a Morris Minor too."

"He had: he had a sister a hairdresser in Kilmallock."

"He had: he had another sister a hairdresser in Ballybunion."

"He had: he was put in a coffin which was put in his father's cart."

"He was: his lady wife sat on top of the coffin driving the donkey."

"She did: Ah, but he was a grand man."

"He was: he was a grand man . . ."

"Good night, Father."

"Good night, Mary."

Hopping round Knock Shrine in
the Falling Rain, 1958

to Karol Wojtyla

When I was thirteen I broke my leg.

Being the sensible, superstitious old lady that she was,
My Aunt Sarah knew that while to know God was good,
To get the ear of his mother was a more practical step:
Kneeling on the flagstone floor of her kitchen, all teaspoons and
　　whins,
Outspoken as Moses, she called out litanies to Our Lady:
The trick was to circumambulate the shrine fifteen times
Repeating the rosary, telling your beads.
And so: that is how I came to be
Hopping round Knock Shrine in the falling rain.

In the heel of that spiritual hunt
I became a falling figure clinging to the shrine wall
While Mayo rain pelleted down, jamming and jetting:
And while all the stalls – of relics, and phials of holy water,
And souvenir grottoes, and souvenir postcards,
And spheres which, when shaken, shook with fairy snow,
And sticks of Knock rock –
Were being folded up for the day, I veered on,
Falling round Knock Shrine in the hopping rain.

Gable, O Gable, is there no Respite to thy Mercy?

The trick did not work
But that is scarcely the point:
That day was a crucial day
In my hedge school of belief,

In the potential of miracle,
In the actuality of vision:
And, therefore, I am grateful
For my plateful
Of hopping round Knock Shrine in the falling rain.

For My Lord Tennyson I Shall Lay Down My Life

to Anthony Cronin

Here at the Mont-Saint-Michel of my master,
At the horn of beaches outside Locksley Hall,
On the farthest and coldest shore
In the June day under pain of night,
I keep at my mind to make it say,
Make it say, make it say,
As his assassins make for me,
The pair of them revolving nearer and nearer
(And yet, between breaths, farther and farther),
Make it say:
"For my Lord Tennyson I shall lay down my life."

I say that—as nearer and nearer they goose-step—
Vanity, and *Gloom* not far behind.
"For my Lord Tennyson I shall lay down my life."

The Death by Heroin of Sid Vicious

There – but for the clutch of luck – go I.

At daybreak – in the arctic fog of a February daybreak –
Shoulder-length helmets in the watchtowers of the
    concentration camp
Caught me out in the intersecting arcs of the swirling
    searchlights.

There were at least a zillion of us caught out there –
Like ladybirds under a boulder –
But under the microscope each of us was unique,

Unique and we broke for cover, crazily breasting
The barbed wire and some of us made it
To the forest edge, but many of us did not

Make it, although their unborn children did –
Such as you whom the camp commandant branded
Sid Vicious of the Sex Pistols. Jesus, break his fall:

There – but for the clutch of luck – go we all.

February 1979

The Crucifixion Circus, Good Friday, Paris, 1981

At the sixth station there was a soft explosion,
And it was not the frantic swish of Veronica's towel
Scouring the face of the gory Christ
Like a pulped prizefighter slumped in his corner.
Perhaps, I thought, it is the man in the porch
With the pistol in his right hand clasped by his left,
Held high above his head pointed into space;
(I had wondered about him on my way in).
It was like the air precipitately being let out of a balloon,
Or the rapid deflation of the bladder of a football.
A tall, saffron-faced lady in long grey skirts,
Barely able to stand on account of her age
Had urinated into her massive black silk drawers –
"My stage curtains," she used to call them to her
    great-grandchildren.
The gold urine trickled slowly, as if patiently, across the stone
    flags,
Delineating a map of Europe on the floor as it trickled –
Trickled until it had become a series of migrations
From Smolensk to Paris;
A urine sample for Doctor God to hold up to the light,
Or to be microscopic about –
A clue to the secret biology of the Universe –
Or for his wastrel son to muck about in.

Her husband gripped her trembling hand
And with his other hand he adjusted the lilac bonnet on her
    head
To make her look more pretty.

That he should think of that at a time like this,
That he should treat his wife with the exact same courtesy
As he did when he was a young man courting a princess,
And that she should crawl forth from her bed
To topple like this,
To bear witness in a public church,
To risk all or nearly,
In order to stand by the side of the subversive Christ,
These are things that do not make me laugh;
These are things that make me weep stone tears.
In spite of the living scandal of the warring churches,
On the map of Europe there is a country of the heart.

Fellow catechumens looked down askance at the floor,
Then up at the radiant, tormented faces of the agèd couple.
Why do people of their age and station
Behave like this – they ought to know better –
At the Stations of the Cross and on – of all days – Good Friday?
We had not yet even arrived at Golgotha Hill:
The old pair did not look as if they intended to budge from the
    pool
In which they stood – out of whose banana-yellow ooze
They flowered and towered like agèd tropical trees,
All wizened and green, all grey and fruity.

The wife kept her eyes fixed on the Cross of Jesus.
Her husband kept his eyes both on her and on the Cross.
Urine or no urine
They were going to bear witness to today's Via Dolorosa
Right out to the end;
If the fellow under the Cross – a dark-skinned young Jew,
Extraordinarily long-haired, even if it is the fashion –
Could himself keep it up to the end. With blood in both eyes
And on his hands and on his feet, he too was in difficulties –

Difficulties with his bodily functions.
Behind the Jew traipsed the priests and the acolytes
In linen albs and lamb's wool surplices:
Voices taunted from the planets: "And where are your assets?"

When at the eleventh station they crucified Christ
The old man held high his head with glittering eyes,
Like a man in the stands at a racecourse
Watching a 20-to-1 winner come home,
His wife holding on to the hem of his raincoat,
Not unused to her husband's gambling coups – a loser in society,
A winner in life. If at night she had a blackout
And forgot to say her prayers (ever since the war she'd been
    having blackouts)
She could always be sure that he would say them for her.
Such things were unspoken of between them
As now they poked their way
In and out the archipelagos and the peninsulas and the lagoons
    of urine,
The rivulets and the puddles,
Until they found the centre aisle
From which they gazed up at the stalagmite organ in the far-off
    loft
Famed for its harpies carved in oak.
During the Stations of the Cross
A family of Germans had been snapping photographs of the
    organ,
With tripod and flash,
Turning their backs on the ludicrous procession-in-progress.

The old man knew that his wife knew what he knew:
That at the end of the war a German soldier
Had hid in the organ loft
In a nest made for him by the sacristy charwoman.

For three weeks he had got away with it until the parish priest –
An armchair general in the French Resistance –
Had flushed him out. The pair of them –
The young German soldier and the young French charwoman –
Were shot in the back of the head – collaborators –
No Jesus Christ to make it a trio, or was there?
The parish priest murmured over his bread and wine
That such things happen, and have to happen, in war.
Just so, just so – murmured a Communist intellectual,
Blood-red wine seeping out of the stained corners of his mouth,
Le Monde for a napkin on his knee.

By now the Crime of the Urine had been doctrinally detected
And the sacristan followed the trail up the centre aisle,
Up and under the organ loft, round by the holy-water font,
Out onto the steps overlooking the Place de la Concorde.
He thought: the guillotine would not be good enough
For people who urinate in churches.
But he consoled himself with the observation that Bonaparte
Had good taste in Egyptian obelisks – painted penises, I should
    think.

In their crusty old rooms
In the mansards overlooking the Madeleine
The two quaking spouses helped each other to undress.
Having laid their two windowsills
With breadcrumbs for the pigeons,
They climbed into bed into one another's arms,
In an exhaustion beyond even their own contemplation –
Beyond the trees and the water, beyond youth and childhood.
He was the first to fall asleep, his eyelids like forest streams,
And the sun – high in the west over the Eiffel Tower and
    St-Cloud –
Framed his golden white-haired face like a face in a shrine,

71

A gaunt embryo in a monstrance.
As sleep came over her she heard him say in his sleep:
"To keep one another warm — warm as urine."
And in Byzantium she saw the gold urine
Mosaicise in her sleep-fog like breath:
A diptych of Madonna and Child — at birth and at death.

The Rose of Blackpool

He was a goalkeeper and I am a postmistress
And the pair of us believed – I say "believed" – in Valentine's
 Day.
What chance had we?
(I speak in hindsight, of course:
I would not have spoken like that in front of the Great Irish Elk
Or, for that matter, in front of a twenty-two-inch colour TV.)
What chance had we?
Every chance – and at the same time not a chance in the world.

You see, I had my own little post office at the very top of
 the hill
And I kept it completely and absolutely empty except for
 the counter.
One day he had said: "You are the Rose of Blackpool";
And that night in bed on my own with my head in the pillow
(*Feathers*, I may say – I cannot abide *foam* –
Nor could *he*)
I whispered to myself: "All right, that's what I'll be,
I'll be – the Rose of Blackpool."

Many's the Valentine's Day that went by
Before I got my hands on a PO of my own
But got it I did – and right on top of the hill!
And in that bare, spic-and-span, unfurnished shop,
With its solitary counter at the very far end,
I stood like a flower in a flowerpot
All the day long – drips and leaves and what-have-ye:
All the year round – "*Number 365, are you still alive?*"

73

And when the door of my PO opened
(And as the years went by, it opened less and less and less, I can
    tell you that)
The doorbell gave out such a ring — such a peal —
That the customer leapt — stood dead — and I smiled
Until my cheeks were redder than even
A Portadown Rose in a Sam McGredy Dream.
And I had my black hair tied up in a bun
And my teeth — well this is what my goalkeeper used say —
Were whiter than the snow in Greece when he played a
Game there in nineteen hundred and fifty-three.
The trouble with my goalkeeper was that he was too good of a
    goalkeeper:
He simply would not let the ball in — not even when you got a
    penalty against him.
Now it sounds Funny Peculiar — and it is —
(But then so is Valentine's Day
And all who steer by the star)
But to be a successful goalkeeper in this world
You simply have to let the odd ball in.
Benny would *not* — and so one night the inevitable happened.
We were up in Dublin and the game was being played under
    lights
And he hit his head off the crossbar making a save
And the two uprights fell across him
And the removals were the next night and the burial was the
    day after.

Of course some people say that he's living in Argentina with a
    white woman.
(I'm brown, by the way, and my name is Conchita.)
But *that's* what *they* say — *what* do *they* know?
I stand alone in my little old lofty and lonely PO,
The Rose of Blackpool,

And I do not believe that there was ever another man in the
    world
Who could court a woman like my goalkeeper courted *me*,
Especially at away matches at nights under lights.
Benny courted Conchita like a fella in a story;
And no matter how many shots he had stopped in the foregoing
    year
He always—oh he always—and he always—
Posted *me* his Valentine.

O Rose of Blackpool, let Mine be always Thine.

The Woman Who Keeps Her Breasts in the Back Garden

Why do you keep your breasts in the back garden?
Well – it's a male-dominated society, isn't it?
Yes, I know it is, but could you explain . . .?
Certainly I'll explain, certainly:
Seeing as how it's a male-dominated society
And there is all this ballyhoo about breasts,
I decided to keep my pair of breasts in the back garden
And once or twice a day I take them out for a walk –
Usually on a leash but sometimes I unleash them –
And they jump up and down and prance a bit
And in that way the males can get their bosom-gaping done
    with
And I can get on with my other activities.
I used to leave them out at night under the glorious stars
But then little men started coming in over the walls.
I have other things on my mind besides my breasts:
Australia – for example – Australia.
To tell you the truth, I think a great deal about Australia.
Thank you very much for talking to us, Miss Delia Fair.

Death in a Graveyard: Père Lachaise

The widow was perching by her husband's grave
When a chestnut dropped down onto her skull;
And she, concussed, dropped down onto her spindly knees,
Her forehead glancing off the sharpness of the kerb:
Dead – before you could say Jack Robinson –
To whom she had been married fifty years:
Mrs Robinson poleaxed by a conker:
How she would have laughed – and so would he:
"There I was – decomposing away like mad –
When you collapsed beside me, bombed by a chestnut."

Strollers remarked upon the old lady asleep
In the noonday sun. And so she slept until dusk
And the keepers discovered her, encircled by cats,
A stone circle of cats around their dead priestess,
She who had fed the strays for fifty years
And who had never quarrelled with her prickly husband,
Yet shared with him laughter
Both of the benign bed and of the shaky street.
Only at mealtimes had they been silent; and silence
They had also shared, as if communing in a foreign tongue.
"Poleaxed by a conker, Jack, at the edge of your grave."
"That's the girl, Jill, jump in quick beside me."

The Golden Girl

Yes, I knew her once – the Golden Girl –
Strange name – she dressed always in black –
Guiding a camel through St Stephen's Green –
Teaching ballet to a farmer in Parnell Square –
Hunting for bus stops at night in O'Connell Street –
Like the gold lunula hanging on the blackthorn tree,
Which was which? Was it the black tree
That, in the dying sun, was the most golden of all?
She was the black tree – the Golden Girl:
And she was called by that name
Because she was what she was –
She walked always in circles in a straight line.

The Golden Girl – and you could say –
Yes, you could say – she had a heart of gold:
Which was why there was always a Gold Rush
Of blokes crazily panning the streets for her:
Yet when one of them – I speak of myself –
Came face to face with her –
Gazing down the gravel of her eyes –
Her heart of gold slipped through my fingers
And her deadpan humour left me standing still:
She was called by that name
Because she was what she was –
She walked always in circles in a straight line.

If you should see her photograph in a magazine
Cut it out – and pencil in the date –
And place it fastidiously in your most coveted book –
Tarry Flynn by Patrick Kavanagh –

But remember that, in spite of her laughing eyes
And her mouth with its puzzled frown,
It bears no resemblance to the actual girl—
To the real Golden Girl
Whom in this life you can only know:
She was called by that name
Because she was what she was—
She walked always in circles in a straight line.

One day Gauguin—or was it Picasso?—
I forget which—it does not matter—
One of the big boys—all his admirers
Round him in the art gallery on whose dirty floor
The Golden Girl knelt with a portfolio of her drawings:
What was evident was not that she was beautiful,
Which she was, but that her drawings—unnoticed—
Were more subtle, more muscular,
Than the works of the big boys, and her eyes were linocuts.
She was called by that name
Because she was what she was—
She walked always in circles in a straight line.

Today it is time to paint the gate
The gate that will not lock.
Today it is time to speak of love—
Love swinging in the wind.
The state has disappeared but she has remained,
And there are no newspapers—only her eyes;
And behind her the sea—the waiting sea:
The sea waiting to enter the city
Like sleep into the head of a child:
And she was called by that name
Because she was what she was—
She walked always in circles in a straight line.

The Children of Hiroshima, Dublin 7

In Prussia Street she bought a house;
A three-storey house with half a roof;
One night we chanced to meet in O'Connell Street;
I enquired if she required help to put back the roof.

We were acquaintances – we were not lovers;
We stood on the roof and ate our lunch;
After nine months she remarked to me:
"Well now that we have got a roof to stand on –

You might like to have a roof over your head:
Would you care to share the same roof as me?
We are total strangers, know each other well,
To me you are just like dirty old bronze."

"Is that a smile on your face?" I said to her:
"Yes, I think it is" – she frowned:
The sky of her face was a fire on the sea:
She ran out the back – "I'm gone to get fags."

II

As I clambered upstairs I had not much time:
In her bedroom I looked at myself in the window:
I saw the mental hospital behind her garden wall:
A kind of football match was going on.

O Jesus – this house is where I yearn to live:
This is the human being with whom I yearn to live:

O Jesus Gypsy – tell me her fate:
Before she comes back through the back-garden gate.

Am I a criminal, awake in the nightmare,
To break into the life of a stranger in Prussia Street?
Jesus – he looked like a Cuban revolutionary – he smiled:
"What's at stake is her heart and not your head."

The football match was upside down:
So upside down that it looked all right:
Then she came back in the door smoking a cigarette:
I stammered: "My name is Joe Cross and I love you."

She waltzed rapidly past me to the mantelpiece:
Flicked the ash of her cigarette into the wrought-iron grate:
Spun around with a smile on the bridge of her nose:
"My name is Nuala Quinn – who are you, strange boy?"

And she threw her arms around me like a slow
Black breeze around a block of flats;
And as we watched the football match in the mental hospital
We sat together on the edge of her bed:

We neither of us were afraid despite the approaching storm:
We exchanged X-ray photographs of each other's scarred
   bodies:
We had no choice but to go back scarred into Eden:
First, to learn how to sit together on the edge of her bed.

III

In Prussia Street there is a house
With a goldfish bowl on the window table:
And on the floor, close up to the ceiling,
Two lovers float, dead as dead can be.

Of what they did die – we do not agree:
"Of romantic love" – the historians lie:
"Of nuclear fallout" – the doctors testify:
"They always kept their windows open" – the neighbours
  whisper.

In the Holy Faith Convent I stab a girl in the back;
In the Christian Brothers' School I slap a boy in the face;
In Eden a priest puts a gun to the head of a nun;
In Hiroshima the bent trees listen to familiar footsteps.

In Prussia Street there is no blue plaque
On the blue house, love, where we did live:
We were against war: we were for blue:
Hiroshima is not, and never was, new!
                    Hiroshima!

World Cup '82

"Just so long as this hotel don't go on fire . . ."
I mumbled as you lay on top of me
In our seventeenth-storey bedroom in Seville:
5.30 a.m. — a new morning already beginning.

Making love in the night in Seville is sweet
But waking up in the morning together is sweeter:
To make sleep with you for the rest of my days,
That is my life's goal now — the cup and the world to me.

We make love with sleeping muscles
We have not used since days of childhood;
In the backs of our arms, in the backs of our legs:
You are my Brazil, and I want you to win.

You permit me to kiss you under each ear
And in the small of your back and on each wrist;
And with your teeth you kiss me on each shoulder
And, smothering my face in the pillow,

Again you recline on me with such spiritual prowess —
Like a feather on a windowsill in a gale.
I whisper: "What makes Brazil unlike every other team?"
You whisper: "They are used to the heat, I suppose."

I want you to beat me twelve goals to nil;
I want you to kick the ball through my net;
I want you to bend me and curl me and chip me;
I want to wear your shirt and you to wear mine.

Making love in the night in Seville is sweet
But waking up in the morning together is sweeter:
To make sleep with you for the rest of my days,
That is my life's goal now – the cup and the world to me.

The Lion Tamer

"Well, what do you work at?" she said to me after about six
 months
Of what a mutual journalist friend was pleased to call our
 "relationship".
"I'm a lion tamer," I replied, off-handedly as possible,
Hoping she'd say: "Are you really?"
Instead she said: "I don't believe you."
I jumped up from my chair and I strode across the room,
Stumbling over a wickerwork magazine rack.
I knelt on one knee at her feet and gazed up at her:
Slowly she edged away from me and backed out the door
And glancing out the window I saw her bounding down the
 road,
Her fair hair gleaming in the wind, her crimson voice growling.
I kicked over a stool and threw my whip on the floor.
What I had hoped for from her was a thorough mauling.
But she preferred artistic types. She had no appetite for lion
 tamers.

Going Home to Meet Sylvia

I

I am going down the road with Sylvia;
And I will not be going home;
I am going down the road with Sylvia;
And I will not be going home.

II

I will be going to the Carnival with Sylvia;
I hope to meet nobody there;
I will be going to the Carnival with Sylvia;
I hope to meet nobody there.

III

I am going down the road to meet Sylvia;
Sylvia is not going to meet me;
I will be coming back down the road from Sylvia;
And I will not be going home.

IV

I am going down the road with Sylvia;
And I will not be going home;
I am going down the road with Sylvia;
And I will not be going home.

The Haulier's Wife Meets Jesus on the Road Near Moone

I live in the town of Cahir,
In the Glen of Aherlow,
Not far from Peekaun
In the townland of Toureen,
At the foot of Galtee Mór
In the County of Tipperary.
I am thirty-three years old,
In the prime of my womanhood:
The mountain stream of my sex
In spate and darkly foaming;
The white hills of my breasts
Brimful and breathing;
The tall trees of my eyes
Screening blue skies;
Yet in each palm of my hand
A sheaf of fallen headstones.
When I stand in profile
Before my bedroom mirror
With my hands on my hips in my slip,
Proud of my body,
Unashamed of my pride,
I appear to myself a naked stranger,
A woman whom I do not know
Except fictionally in the looking-glass,
Quite dramatically beautiful.
Yet in my soul I yearn for affection,
My soul is empty for the want of affection.
I am married to a haulier,
A popular and a wealthy man,

An alcoholic and a county councillor,
Father with me of four sons,
By repute a sensitive man and he is
Except when he makes love to me:
He takes leave of his senses,
Handling me as if I were a sack of gravel
Or a carnival dummy,
A fruit machine or a dodgem.
He makes love to me about twice a year;
Thereafter he does not speak to me for weeks,
Sometimes not for months.
One night in Cruise's Hotel in Limerick
I whispered to him: Please *take* me.
(We had been married five years
And we had two children.)
Christ, do you know what he said?
Where? Where do you want me to take you?
And he rolled over and fell asleep,
Tanked up with seventeen pints of beer.
We live in a Georgian, Tudor, Classical Greek,
Moorish, Spanish Hacienda, Regency Period,
Ranch House, Three-Storey Bungalow
On the edge of the edge of town:
"Poor Joe's Row"
The townspeople call it,
But our real address is "Ronald Reagan Hill" –
That vulturous-looking man in the States.
We're about twelve miles from Ballyporeen
Or, as the vulture flies, about eight miles.
After a month or two of silence
He says to me: Wife, I'm sorry;
I know that we should be separated,
Annulled or whatever,
But on account of the clients and the neighbours,

Not to mention the children, it is plain
As a pikestaff we are glued to one another
Until death do us part.
Why don't you treat yourself
To a weekend up in Dublin,
A night out at the theatre:
I'll pay for the whole shagging lot.

There was a play on at the time
In the Abbey Theatre in Dublin
Called *The Gigli Concert*,
And, because I liked the name —
But also because it starred
My favourite actor, Tom Hickey —
I telephoned the Abbey from Cahir.
They had but one vacant seat left!
I was so thrilled with myself,
And at the prospect of Tom Hickey
In a play called *The Gigli Concert*
(Such a euphonious name for a play, I thought),
That one wet day I drove over to Clonmel
And I went wild, and I bought a whole new outfit.
I am not one bit afraid to say
That I spent all of £200 on it
(Not, of course, that Tom Hickey would see me
But I'd be seeing myself seeing Tom Hickey
Which would be almost, if not quite,
The very next best thing):
A long, tight-fitting, black skirt
Of Chinese silk,
With matching black jacket
And lace-frilled, pearl-white blouse;
Black fishnet stockings with sequins;
Black stiletto high-heeled shoes

Of pure ostrich leather.
I thought to myself – subconsciously, of course –
If I don't transpose to be somebody's *femme fatale*
It won't anyhow be for the want of trying.

Driving up to Dublin I began to daydream
And either at Horse & Jockey or Abbeyleix
I took a wrong turn and within a quarter of an hour
I knew I was lost. I stopped the car
And I asked the first man I saw on the road
For directions:
"Follow me" – he said – "my name is Jesus:
Have no fear of me – I am a travelling actor.
We'll have a drink together in the nearby inn."
It turned out we were on the road near Moone.
(Have you ever been to the Cross at Moone?
Once my children and I had a picnic at Moone
When they were little and we were on one
Of our Flight into Egypt jaunts to Dublin.
They ran round the High Cross round and round
As if it were a maypole, which maybe it is:
Figure carvings of loaves and fishes, lions and dolphins.
I drank black coffee from a thermos flask
And the children drank red lemonade
And they were wearing blue duffle coats with red scarves
And their small, round, laughing, freckled faces
Looked pointedly like the faces of the twelve apostles
Gazing out at us from the plinth of the Cross
Across a thousand years.
Only, of course, their father was not with us:
He was busy – busy being our family euphemism.
(Every family in Ireland has its own family euphemism
Like a heraldic device or a coat of arms.)
Jesus turned out to be a lovely man,

All that a woman could ever possibly dream of:
Gentle, wild, soft-spoken, courteous, sad;
Angular, awkward, candid, methodical;
Humorous, passionate, angry, kind;
Entirely sensitive to a woman's world.
Discreetly I invited Jesus to spend the night with me —
Stay with me, the day is almost over and it is getting dark —
But he waved me aside with one wave of his hand,
Not contemptuously, but compassionately.
"Our night will come," he smiled,
And he resumed chatting about my children,
All curiosity for their welfare and well-being.
It was like a fire burning in me when he talked to me.
There was only one matter I felt guilty about
And that was my empty vacant seat in the Abbey.
At closing time he kissed me on both cheeks
And we bade one another goodbye and then —
Just as I had all but given up hope —
He kissed me full on the mouth,
My mouth wet with alizarin lipstick
(A tube of Guerlain 4 which I've had for twelve years).
As I drove on into Dublin to the Shelbourne Hotel
I kept hearing his Midlands voice
Saying to me over and over, across the Garden of Gethsemane —
Our night will come.

Back in the town of Cahir,
In the Glen of Aherlow,
Not far from Peekaun
In the townland of Toureen,
At the foot of Galtee Mór
In the County of Tipperary,
For the sake of something to say
In front of our four sons

My husband said to me:
Well, what was Benjamino Gigli like?
Oh, 'twas a phenomenal concert!
And what was Tom Hickey like?
Miraculous — I whispered — miraculous.
Our night will come — he had smiled — our night will come.

Bewley's Oriental Café,
Westmoreland Street

When she asked me to keep an eye on her things
I told her I'd be glad to keep an eye on her things.
While she breakdanced off to the ladies' loo
I concentrated on keeping an eye on her things.
What are you doing? a Security Guard growled,
His moustache gnawing at the beak of his peaked cap.
When I told him that a young woman whom I did not know
Had asked me to keep an eye on her things, he barked:
Instead of keeping an eye on the things
Of a young woman whom you do not know,
Keep an eye on your own things.
I put my two hands on his hips and squeezed him:
Look — for me the equivalent of the Easter Rising
Is to be accosted by a woman whom I do not know
And asked by her to keep an eye on her things;
On her medieval backpack and on her space-age Walkman;
Calm down and cast aside your peaked cap
And take down your trousers and take off your shoes
And I will keep an eye on your things also.
Do we not cherish all the children of the nation equally?
That young woman does not know the joy she has given me
By asking me if I would keep an eye on her things;
I feel as if I am on a Dart to Bray,
Keeping an eye on her things;
More radical than being on the pig's back,
Keeping an eye on nothing.
The Security Guard made a heap on the floor
Of his pants and shoes,
Sailing his peaked cap across the café like a frisbee.

His moustache sipped at a glass of milk.
It is as chivalrous as it is transcendental
To be sitting in Bewley's Oriental Café
With a naked Security Guard,
Keeping an eye on his things
And on old ladies
With, under their palaeolithic oxters, thousands of loaves of
    coarse brown bread.

Man Smoking a Cigarette in the Barcelona Metro

I was standing in the Metro in the Plaza de Cataluña
Waiting for the rush-hour train to take me home to Tibidabo
When, gazing and staring – as one does gaze and stare –
At the passengers on the opposite platform,
I saw a naked man smoking a cigarette.
I cannot tell you how shocked I was.
He was by no means the only passenger smoking a cigarette
But he was the only naked passenger smoking a cigarette.
It was like seeing a horse in the rush hour smoking in the
    crowd.
Although I was in a hurry to get home to Tibidabo
I was so shocked that I ran back down the stairs,
Past the buskers and the jasmine-sellers and the Guardia Civil,
And crossed the tunnel to the other side of the tracks.
I went straight up to him and with no beating about the bush
I expressed to him my indignation and my ideological position:
"I happen to regard the naked human body as sacred –
If you want to profane it by smoking a cigarette
Have the decency to put on some clothes
And go about your smoking like everyone else
In shame and concealment, in jeans and ponchos.
What do you think clothes are for but to provide an alibi
For perversity, a cover-up for unnatural practices?"
He snatched the cigarette from his mouth and threw it down
    into the tracks,
And immediately he looked like a human being
    metamorphosed –
He began to quake with laughter, whinnying, neighing –
As if he were the first horse on earth,

Sauntering up and down the platform of the Metro
All knees and neck,
The bells of his genitals tolling in the groin of time.
As he rode up and down the platform,
In ones and twos and threes the women passengers
Began to fling their smoking cigarettes down into the tracks
And, as they did,
Their garments fell away from them
And they stepped out into themselves cigaretteless,
As with a newborn sense of pride and attraction.
In the end only all the men were left—
Fuming aliens—
Chain-smoking in their clobber,
Glaring with clumsy envy
At the naked man, cigaretteless,
Circled round by all of his newly equipped fans
Fanning him with nothing but the fans of their bodies
Riding high on thigh-bone and wrist:
No longer hooked on trains, or appearances, or loss.

The Cabinet Table

Alice Gunn is a cleaner woman
Down at Government Buildings,
And after seven o'clock Mass last night
(Isn't it a treat to be able to go to Sunday Mass
On a Saturday! To sit down to Saturday Night TV
Knowing you've fulfilled your Sunday obligation!)
She came back over to The Flats for a cup of tea
(I offered her sherry but she declined –
Oh, I never touch sherry on a Saturday night –
Whatever she meant by that, I don't know).
She had us all in stitches, telling us
How one afternoon after a Cabinet Meeting
She got one of the security men
To lie down on the Cabinet Table,
And what she didn't do to him –
And what she did do to him –
She didn't half tell us;
But she told us enough to be going on with.
"Do you know what it is?" she says to me:
"No," says I, "what is it?"
"It's mahogany," she says, "pure mahogany."

10.30 a.m. Mass, 16 June 1985

When the priest made his entrance on the altar on the stroke of
    10.30,
He looked like a film star at an international airport
After having flown in from the other side of the world,
As if the other side of the world was the other side of the street;
Only, instead of an overnight bag slung over his shoulder,
He was carrying the chalice in its triangular green veil –
The way a dapper comedian cloaks a dove in a silk
    handkerchief.
Having kissed the altar, he strode over to the microphone:
I'd like to say how glad I am to be here with you this morning.

Oddly, you could see quite well that he was genuinely glad –
As if, in fact, he had been actually looking forward to this
    Sunday service,
Much the way I had been looking forward to it myself;
As if, in fact, this was the big moment of his day – of his week,
Not merely another ritual to be sanctimoniously performed.
He was a small, stocky, handsome man in his forties
With a big mop of curly grey hair
And black, horn-rimmed, tinted spectacles.
I am sure that more than half the women in the church
Fell in love with him on the spot –
Not to mention the men.
The reading from the prophet Ezekiel (17: 22–24)
Was a piece about cedar trees in Israel,
The epistle was St Paul.
With the Gospel, however, things began to look up –

The parable of the mustard seed as being the kingdom of
    heaven;
Now, then, the homily, at best probably inoffensively boring.

It's Father's Day – this small, solid, serious, sexy priest began –
And I want to tell you about my own father
Because none of you knew him.
If there was one thing he liked, it was a pint of Guinness;
If there was one thing he liked more than a pint of Guinness
It was two pints of Guinness.
But then when he was fifty-five he gave up drink.
I never knew why, but I had my suspicions.
Long after he had died my mother told me why:
He was so proud of me when I entered the seminary
That he gave up drinking as his way of thanking God.
But he himself never said a word about it to me –
He kept his secret to the end. He died from cancer
A few weeks before I was ordained a priest.
I'd like to go to Confession – he said to me:
OK – I'll go and get a priest – I said to him:
No – don't do that – I'd prefer to talk to *you*.
Dying, he confessed to me the story of his life.
How many of you here at Mass today are fathers?
I want all of you who are fathers to stand up.

Not one male in transept or aisle or nave stood up –
It was as if all the fathers in the church had been caught out
In the profanity of their sanctity,
In the bodily nakedness of their fatherhood,
In the carnal deed of their fathering;
Then, in ones and twos and threes, fifty or sixty of us clambered
    to our feet
And blushed to the roots of our being.

Now—declared the priest—let the rest of us
Praise these men our fathers.
He began to clap hands.
Gradually the congregation began to clap hands,
Until the entire church was ablaze with clapping hands—
Wives vying with daughters, sons with sons,
Clapping clapping clapping clapping clapping,
While I stood there in a trance, tears streaming down my
    cheeks:
Jesus!
I want to tell you about my own father
Because none of you knew him!

Hymn to a Broken Marriage

Dear Nessa – Now that our marriage is over
I would like you to know that, if I could put back the clock
Fifteen years to the cold March day of our wedding,
I would wed you again and, if that marriage also broke,
I would wed you yet again and, if it a third time broke,
Wed you again, and again, and again, and again, and again:
If you would have me which, of course, you would not.
For, even you – in spite of your patience and your innocence
(Strange characteristics in an age such as our own) –
Even you require to shake off the addiction of romantic love
And seek, instead, the herbal remedy of a sane affection
In which are mixed in profuse and fair proportion
Loverliness, brotherliness, fatherliness:
A sane man could not espouse a more intimate friend than you.

The Jewish Bride

AFTER REMBRANDT

At the black canvas of estrangement,
As the smoke empties from the ruins under a gold winter sky,
Death-trains clattering across the back gardens of Amsterdam –
Sheds, buckets, wire, concrete,
Manholes, pumps, pliers, scaffolding –
I see, as if for the first time, –
The person you were, and are, and always will be
Despite the evil that men do:
The teenage girl on the brink of womanhood
Who, when I met you, was on the brink of everything –
Composing fairytales and making drawings
That used remind your friends of Anderson and Thurber –
Living your hidden life that promised everything
Despite all the maimed, unreliable men and women
Who were at that moment congregating all around you:
Including, of course, most of all, myself.
You made of your bedroom a flowing stream
Into which, daily, you threw proofs of your dreams;
Pinned to your bedroom wall with brass-studded drawing pins
Newspaper and magazine photographs of your heroes and
    heroines.
People who met you breathed the air of freedom,
And sensuality fragile as it was wild:
"Nessa's air makes free," people used say,
Like in the dark ages, "Town air makes free."
The miracle is that you survived me.
You stroll about the malls and alleyways of Amsterdam,
About its islands and bridges, its archways and jetties,
With spring in your heels, although it is winter;

Privately, publicly, along the Grand Parade;
A Jewish Bride who has survived the death camp,
Free at last of my swastika eyes
Staring at you from across spiked dinner plates
Or from out of the bunker of a TV armchair;
Free of the glare off my jackboot silence;
Free of the hysteria of my gestapo voice;
Now your shyness replenished with all your old cheeky
    confidence –
That grassy well at which red horses used rear up and sip
With young men naked riding bareback calling your name.
Dog-muzzle of tension torn down from your face;
Black polythene of asphyxiation peeled away from your soul;
Your green eyes quivering with dark, sunny laughter
And – all spreadeagled and supple again – your loving, freckled
    hands.

Around the Corner from Francis Bacon

Around the corner from Francis Bacon
Was where we made our first nest together
On the waters of the flood;
Where we first lived in sin:
The sunniest, most virtuous days of our life.
Not even the pastoral squalor of Clapham Common,
Nor the ghetto life of Notting Hill Gate,
Nor the racial drama of Barcelona,
Nor the cliffhanging bourgeois life of Cork City
Could ever equal those initial, primeval times together
Living in sin
In the halcyon ambience of South Kensington,
A haven for peaceful revolutionaries such as Harriet Waugh
Or Francis Bacon, or ourselves.
I slept on an ironing board in the kitchen
And you slept in the attic:
Late at night when all the other flat-dwellers
Were abed and – we thought wishfully – asleep,
You crept down the attic ladder
To make love with me on the ironing board,
As if we had known each other in a previous life
So waterily did our two body-phones attune,
Underwater swimming face to face in the dark,
Francis Bacon-Cimabue style.
My body-phone was made in Dublin
But your body-phone was made in Japan.
Standing up naked on the kitchen floor,
In the smog-filtered moonlight,
You placed your hand on my little folly, murmuring:

I have come to iron you, Sir Board.
Far from the tyrant liberties of Dublin, Ireland,
Where the comedy of freedom was by law forbidden
And truth, since the freedom of the State, gone underground.
When you had finished ironing me
I felt like hot silk queueing up to be bathèd
Under a waterfall in Samarkand
Or a mountain stream in Enniskerry.
Every evening I waited for you to come home,
Nipping out only in the rush hour to the delicatessen
Where Francis Bacon, basket under arm,
Surfacing like Mr Mole from his mews around the corner,
Used be stocking up in tomato purée and curry powder
Before heading off into the night and The Colony Room Club
Into whose green dark you and I sometimes also tiptoed.
In your own way you were equally Beatrix Potter-like,
Coming home to me laden with fish fingers and baked beans.
While I read to you from Dahlberg, you taught me about the
    psyche
Of the female orang-outang caged in the zoo:
Coronation Street . . . Z Cars . . . The World in Action . . .
Then Z Cars to beat all Z Cars – our own world in action –
The baskets of your eyes chock-a-block with your unique
    brands
Of tomato purée and curry powder;
Or, *That Was The Week That Was*, and then, my sleeping
    friend,
In the sandhills of whose shoulders sloping secretly down
Into small, hot havens of pure unscathèd sands
Where the only sounds are the sounds of the sea's tidal waters
Flooding backwards and forwards,
Tonight is the night that always is forever –
Ten or twenty minutes in the dark,
And in four million years or so

My stomach will swarm again suddenly with butterflies,
As with your bowl of water and your towel,
Your candle and your attic ladder,
Your taut high wire and your balancing pole,
A green minidress over your arm, a Penguin paperback in your
      hand,
I watch you coming towards me in the twilight of rush hour
On your hands and knees
And on the wet, mauve tip of your extended tongue
The two multicoloured birds of your plumed eyes ablaze
Around the corner from Francis Bacon.

Raymond of the Rooftops

The morning after the night
The roof flew off the house
And our sleeping children narrowly missed
Being decapitated by falling slates,
I asked my husband if he would
Help me put back the roof:
But no – he was too busy at his work
Writing for a women's magazine in London
An Irish fairytale called *Raymond of the Rooftops.*
Will you have a heart, woman – he bellowed –
Can't you see I am up to my eyes and ears in work,
Breaking my neck to finish *Raymond of the Rooftops,*
Fighting against time to finish *Raymond of the Rooftops,*
Putting everything I have got into *Raymond of the Rooftops?*

Isn't is well for him? *Everything he has got!*

All I wanted him to do was to stand
For an hour, maybe two hours, three at the most,
At the bottom of the stepladder
And hand me up slates while I slated the roof:
But no – once again I was proving to be the insensitive,
Thoughtless, feckless even, wife of the artist.
There was I up to my fat, raw knees in rainwater
Worrying him about the hole in our roof
While he was up to his neck in *Raymond of the Rooftops.*
Will you have a heart, woman – he bellowed –
Can't you see I am up to my eyes and ears in work,
Breaking my neck to finish *Raymond of the Rooftops,*

Fighting against time to finish *Raymond of the Rooftops*,
Putting everything I have got into *Raymond of the Rooftops*?

Isn't it well for him? *Everything he has got!*

The Turkish Carpet

No man could have been more unfaithful
To his wife than me;
Scarcely a day passed
That I was not unfaithful to her.
I would be in the living room ostensibly reading or writing
When she'd come home from work unexpectedly early
And, popping her head round the door, find me wrapped round
A figure of despair.
It would not have been too bad if I'd been wrapped round
Another woman – that would have been infidelity of a kind
With which my wife could have coped.
What she could not cope with, try as she did,
Was the infidelity of unhope,
The personal betrayal of universal despair.
When my wife called to me from the living-room door
Tremblingly ajar, with her head peering round it –
The paintwork studded with headwounds and knuckleprints –
Called to me across the red, red grass of home –
The Turkish Carpet –
Which her gay mother had given us as a wedding present
(And on which our children had so often played
Dolls' houses on their hands and knees
And headstands and cartwheels and dances,
And on which we ourselves had so often made love),
I clutched my despair to my breast
And with brutality kissed it – Sweet Despair –
Staring red-eyed down at *The Turkish Carpet*.
O my dear husband, will you not be faithful to me?
Have I not given you hope all the days of my life?

The Pietà's Over

The Pietà's over – and, now, my dear, droll husband,
As middle age tolls its bell along the via dolorosa of life,
It is time for you to get down off my knees
And learn to walk on your own two feet.
I will admit it is difficult for a man of forty
Who has spent all his life reclining in his wife's lap,
Being given birth to by her again and again, year in, year out,
To stand on his own two feet, but it has to be done –
Even if at the end of the day he commits hari-kari.
A man cannot be a messiah for ever,
Messiahing about in his wife's lap,
Suffering fluently in her arms,
Flowing up and down in the lee of her bosom,
Forever being mourned for by the eternal feminine,
Being keened over every night of the week for sixty mortal
    years.

The Pietà's over – it is Easter over all our lives:
The revelation of our broken marriage, and its resurrection;
The breaking open of the tomb, and the setting free.
Painful as it was for me, I put you down off my knee
And I showed you the door.
Although you pleaded with me to keep you on my knee
And to mollycoddle you, humour you, within the family circle
("Don't put me out into the cold world," you cried),
I did not take the easy way out and yield to you.
Instead I took down the door off its hinges
So that the sunlight shone all the more squarely
Upon the pure, original brokenness of our marriage;

I whispered to you, quietly, yet audibly,
For all the diaspora of your soul to hear:
The Pietà's over.

Yet even now, one year later, you keep looking back
From one side of Europe to the other,
Gaping at my knees as if my knees
Were the source of all that you have been, are, or will be.
By all means look around you, but stop looking back.
I would not give you shelter if you were homeless in the streets
For you must make your home in yourself, not in a woman.
Keep going out the road for it is only out there –
Out there where the river achieves its riverlessness –
That you and I can become at last strangers to one another,
Ready to join up again on Resurrection Day.
Therefore, I must keep whispering to you, over and over:
My dear loved one, I have to tell you,
You have run the gamut of piety –
The Pietà's over.

Six Nuns Die in Convent Inferno

To the
happy memory of six Loreto nuns
who died
between midnight and morning of
2 June 1986

I

We resided in a Loreto convent in the centre of Dublin city
On the east side of a public gardens, St Stephen's Green.
Grafton Street – the *paseo*
Where everybody *paseo*'d, including even ourselves –
Debouched on the north side, and at the top of Grafton Street,
Or round the base of the great patriotic pebble of O'Donovan
　　Rossa,
Knelt tableaus of punk girls and punk boys.
When I used pass them – scurrying as I went –
Often as not to catch a mass in Clarendon Street,
The Carmelite Church in Clarendon Street
(Myself, I never used the Clarendon Street entrance,
I always slipped in by way of Johnson's Court,
Opposite the side entrance to Bewley's Oriental Café),
I could not help but smile, as I sucked on a Fox's mint,
That for all the half-shaven heads and the martial garb
And the dyed hair-dos and the nappy pins
They looked so conventional, really, and vulnerable,
Clinging to warpaint and to uniforms and to one another.
I knew it was myself who was the ultimate drop-out,
The delinquent, the recidivist, the vagabond,
The wild woman, the subversive, the original punk.
Yet, although I confess I was smiling, I was also afraid,
Appalled by my own nerve, my own fervour,

112

My apocalyptic enthusiasm, my other-worldly hubris:
To opt out of the world and to
Choose such exotic loneliness,
Such terrestrial abandonment,
A lifetime of bicycle lamps and bicycle pumps,
A lifetime of galoshes stowed under the stairs,
A lifetime of umbrellas drying out in the kitchens.

I was an old nun – an agèd beadswoman –
But I was no daw.
I knew what a weird bird I was, I knew that when we
Went to bed we were as eerie an aviary as you'd find
In all the blown-off rooftops of the city:
Scuttling about our dorm, wheezing, shrieking, croaking,
In our yellowy corsets, wonky suspenders, strung-out garters,
A bony crew in the gods of the sleeping city.
Many's the night I lay awake in bed
Dreaming what would befall us if there were a fire:
No fire-escapes outside, no fire-extinguishers inside;
To coin a Dublin saying,
We'd not stand a snowball's chance in hell. Fancy that!
It seemed too good to be true:
Happy death vouchsafed only to the few.
Sleeping up there was like sleeping at the top of the mast
Of a nineteenth-century schooner, and in the daytime
We old nuns were the ones who crawled out on the yardarms
To stitch and sew the rigging and the canvas.
To be sure we were weird birds, oddballs, Christniks,
For we had done the weirdest thing a woman can do –
Surrendered the marvellous passions of girlhood,
The innocent dreams of childhood,
Not for a night or a weekend or even a Lent or a season,
But for a lifetime.
Never to know the love of a man or a woman;

Never to have children of our own;
Never to have a home of our own;
All for why and for what?
To follow a young man – would you believe it –
Who lived two thousand years ago in Palestine
And who died a common criminal strung up on a tree.

As we stood there in the disintegrating dormitory
Burning to death in the arms of Christ –
O Christ, Christ, come quickly, quickly –
Fluttering about in our tight, gold bodices,
Beating our wings in vain,
It reminded me of the snaps one of the sisters took
When we took a seaside holiday in 1956
(The year Cardinal Mindszenty went into hiding
In the US legation in Budapest.
He was a great hero of ours, Cardinal Mindszenty,
Any of us would have given our right arm
To have been his nun – darning his socks, cooking his meals,
Making his bed, doing his washing and ironing.)
Somebody – an affluent buddy of the bishop's repenting his
    affluence –
Loaned Mother Superior a secluded beach in Co. Waterford –
Ardmore, along the coast from Tramore –
A cove with palm trees, no less, well off the main road.
There we were, fluttering up and down the beach,
Scampering hither and thither in our starched bathing-costumes.
Tonight, expiring in the fire, was quite much like that,
Only instead of scampering into the waves of the sea,
Now we were scampering into the flames of the fire.

That was one of the gayest days of my life,
The day the sisters went swimming.
Often in the silent darkness of the chapel after Benediction,

During the Exposition of the Blessed Sacrament,
I glimpsed the sea again as it was that day.
Praying – daydreaming really –
I became aware that Christ is the ocean
Forever rising and falling on the world's shore.
Now tonight in the convent Christ is the fire in whose waves
We are doomed but delighted to drown.
And, darting in and out of the flames of the dormitory,
Gabriel, with that extraordinary message of his on his boyish
    lips,
Frenetically pedalling his skybike.
He whispers into my ear what I must do
And I do it – and die.
Each of us in our own tiny, frail, furtive way
Was a Mother of God, mothering forth illegitimate Christs
In the street life of Dublin city.
God have mercy on our whirring souls –
Wild women were we all –
And on the misfortunate, poor fire-brigade men
Whose task it will be to shovel up our ashes and shovel
What is left of us into black plastic refuse sacks.
Fire-brigade men are the salt of the earth.

Isn't it a marvellous thing how your hour comes
When you least expect it? When you lose a thing,
Not to know about it until it actually happens?
How, in so many ways, losing things is such a refreshing
    experience,
Giving you a sense of freedom you've not often experienced?
How lucky I was to lose – I say, lose – lose my life.
It was a Sunday night, and after vespers
I skipped bathroom so that I could hop straight into bed
And get in a bit of a read before lights out:
Conor Cruise O'Brien's new book *The Siege*,

All about Israel and superlatively insightful
For a man who they say is reputedly an agnostic—
I got a loan of it from the brother-in-law's married niece—
But I was tired out and I fell asleep with the book open
Face down across my breast and I woke
To the racket of bellowing flame and snarling glass.
The first thing I thought was that the brother-in-law's married
    niece
Would never again get her Conor Cruise O'Brien back
And I had seen on the price-tag that it cost £23.00:
Small wonder that the custom of snipping off the price
As an exercise in social deportment has simply died out;
Indeed a book today is almost worth buying for its price,
Its price frequently being more remarkable than its contents.

The strange Eucharist of my death—
To be eaten alive by fire and smoke.
I clasped the dragon to my breast
And stroked his red-hot ears.
Strange! There we were, all sleeping molecules,
Suddenly all giving birth to our deaths,
All frantically in labour.
Doctors and midwives weaved in and out
In gowns of smoke and gloves of fire.
Christ, like an Orthodox patriarch in his dressing-gown,
Flew up and down the dormitory, splashing water on our souls:
Sister Eucharia; Sister Seraphia; Sister Rosario;
Sister Gonzaga; Sister Margaret; Sister Edith.
If you will remember us—six nuns burnt to death—
Remember us for the frisky girls that we were,
Now more than ever kittens in the sun.

When Jesus heard these words at the top of Grafton Street
Uttered by a small, agèd, emaciated, female punk
Clad all in mourning black, and grieving like an alley cat,
He was annulled with astonishment, and turning round
He declared to the gangs of teenagers and dicemen following
    him:
"I tell you, not even in New York City
Have I found faith like this."

That night in St Stephen's Green,
After the keepers had locked the gates,
And the courting couples had found cinemas themselves to
    die in,
The six nuns who had died in the convent inferno,
From the bandstand they'd been hiding under, crept out
And knelt together by the Fountain of the Three Fates,
Reciting the Agnus Dei: reciting it as if it were the torch song
Of all aid—Live Aid, Self Aid, AIDS, and All Aid—
Lord, I am not worthy
That thou should'st enter under my roof;
Say but the word and my soul shall be healed.

The Rape of Europa

AFTER TITIAN

to Seamus and Marie

"Is life a dream" – my sleeping daughter beseeches me,
Gaping up at me anxiously out of the ashes of her sleep
As I bend down low over her to kiss her goodnight –
"I was playing on the shore with the other girls,
Under the cliff where the Car Assembly Works is,
When the man who works in Mr Conway's field,
The big fellow who lives alone and who always says hallo,
Casually came striding towards us through the barbed wire,
The muscles in his arms bubbling in the sun
As if the empty sandhills were packed stadia,
And his body – he had left off all his clothes –
Was a nude of crimson triangles of blood,
Where the barbs had pierced his snow-white flesh;
The other girls began to cry –
I do not know why I did not also begin to cry,
Only I thought he looked quite beautiful the way he was.
The more I gazed into his grassy eyes
The more his wounds from the barbed wire appeared to teem,
Until curly hair sprouted from each wound, and big floppy ears,
And his mouth and nostrils became one large, wet, slithery
    snout,
And when he leaned over towards me, putting his two hands
On the yellow sand, they changed into hooves,
And two legs fell down slowly out of his backside
With a thin, smiling tail the length of a clothesline.
He curled up on the sand and he looked so forlorn
I thought of how I would like to go to sleep on his back
And caress his hide with my hand round his horn

And pillow my face in his shoulderblades
And float off across the ocean to the Island of Bulls
In whose blue and red skies
I could see astronaut babies cascading in embryos.
And when I asked him if he would give me a ride
He lowed as if the dusk was a towel on his brow
And I put flowers on his head,
Flowers which I had been gathering with the other girls
In the seaside meadows among the hills of fern —
Wild rose, yellow crocus, narcissus, violet, hyacinth —
And just then as I mounted him you came into my bedroom
And I looked up and I saw you
Bending down low over me to kiss me goodnight.
"Life is a dream, Papa, isn't it? Life is a dream?"

"Life is a dream, Phoenix, life is a dream.
Go back to sleep now and have a wild ride on your bull
For there's only noise to lose when quietude is on the rampage.
Dream is life's element and symbol — as the sea's the eel's;
We expire if we're deprived of our element and symbol.
Smeared, daubed, licked, bloodied in entrails of dream.
If the bull has loosed the paddock of his flesh it means
That boys might once more again be boys and girls girls,
Not entrepreneurs and shareholders in the Car Assembly Works,
To be assessed and calculated in the files of newspapers.
When you wake up in the morning
Before you brush your teeth, before even you say your prayers,
Turn over on your back and count
The big fellow who works in Mr Conway's field
As you count sheep when you're going to sleep;
Count all the babies who have never been born
As well as all the babies who have been born.
If you're late for school, I'll write a note for teacher.
Sleep, Phoenix, sleep."

The Hay-Carrier

AFTER VERONICA BOLAY

Have you ever saved hay in Mayo in the rain?
Have you ever made hay in Mayo in the sun?
Have you ever carried above your head a haycock on a
　　pitchfork?
Have you ever slept in a haybarn on the road from Mayo into
　　Egypt?
I am a hay-carrier.
My father was a hay-carrier.
My mother was a hay-carrier.
My brothers were hay-carriers.
My sisters were hay-carriers.
My wife is a hay-carrier.
My son is a hay-carrier.
His sons are hay-carriers.
His daughters are hay-carriers.
We were always all hay-carriers.
We will always be hay-carriers.
For the great gate of night stands painted red—
And all of heaven lies waiting to be fed.

The Divorce Referendum, Ireland, 1986

By the time the priest started into his sermon
I was adrift on a leaf of tranquillity,
Feeling only the need and desire to praise,
To feed praise to the tiger of life.
Hosanna, Hosanna, Hosanna.
He was a gentle-voiced, middle-aged man,
Slightly stooped under a gulf of grey hair,
Slightly tormented by an excess of humility.
He talked felicitously of the Holy Spirit –
As if he really believed in what he was preaching –
Not as if he was aiming to annotate a diagram
Or to sub-edit the gospel,
But as if the Holy Spirit was real as rainwater.
Then his voice changed colour –
You could see it change from pink into white.
He rasped: "It is the wish of the Hierarchy
That today the clergy of Ireland put before you
Christ's teaching on the indissolubility of marriage
And to remind you that when you vote in the Divorce
    Referendum
The Church's teaching and Christ's teaching are one and the
    same."
Stunned, I stared up at him from my pew
As he stood there supported by candles and gladioli,
Vestments, and altarboys at his feet;
I could feel my breastplate tighten and my shoulderblades
    quiver;
I knew the anger that Jesus Christ felt
When he drove from the temple the traders and stockbrokers.

I have come into this temple today to pray
And be healed by, and joined with, the Spirit of Life,
Not to be invaded by ideology.
I say unto you, preacher and orators of the Hierarchy,
Do not bring ideology into my house of prayer.

I closed my eyes
And I did not open them again until I could hear
The priest murmuring the prayers of the Consecration.
At Holy Communion I kept my eyes on a small girl
To whom the priest had to bend low to give her the host.
Curtseying, she smiled eagerly, and flew back down the aisle,
Carrying in her breast the Eucharist of her innocence:
May she have children of her own
And as many husbands as will praise her –
For what are husbands for, but to praise their wives?

What Shall I Wear, Darling,
to *The Great Hunger*?

"What shall I wear, darling, to *The Great Hunger*?"
She shrieked at me helplessly from the east bedroom
Where the west wind does be blowing betimes.
I did not hesitate to hazard a spontaneous response:
"Your green evening gown –
Your see-through, sleeveless, backless, green evening gown."
We arrived at the Peacock
In good time for everybody to have a good gawk at her
Before the curtain went up on *The Great Hunger*.
At the interval everybody was clucking about, cooing
That it was simply stunning – her dress –
"Darling, you look like Mother Divinity in your see-through,
Sleeveless, backless, green evening gown – it's so visual!"
At the party after the show – simply everybody was there –
Winston Lenihan, Consolata O'Carroll-Riviera, Yves St
     Kirkegaard –
She was so busy being admired that she forgot to get drunk.
But the next morning it was business as usual –
Grey serge pants, blue donkey jacket – driving around Dolphin's
     Barn
In her Opel Kadett hatchback
Checking up on the rents. "All these unmarried young
     mothers
And their frogspawn, living on the welfare –
You would think that it never occurs to them
That it's their rents that pay for the outfits I have to wear
Whenever *The Great Hunger* is playing at the Peacock.
No, it never occurs to them that in Ireland today
It is not easy to be a landlord and a patron of the arts.

It is not for nothing that we in Fail Gael have a social
    conscience:
Either you pay the shagging rent or you get out on the street.
Next week I have to attend three-and-a-half *Great Hungers*,
Not to mention a half-dozen *Juno and the Paycocks*."

EI Flight 106: New York–Dublin

AFTER J. M. W. TURNER

There was an empty seat between us as the jumbo began to taxi
And she – a craggy girl of about seventy-five years of age –
Leaned over and whispered conspiratorially, huskily:
"We've got an empty seat to ourselves – between ourselves."
She winked, all her wing-flaps trembling,
Slashes of eyeshadow, daubs of rouge,
Her eyes roving around in their sockets as they scoured me
For what pusillanimous portions of manhood I might possess.
She exuded femininity as an elephant exudes hide:
Wearing all of her seventy-five years as ethereally
As an adolescent girl wearing earrings.
"We've got an empty seat to ourselves," she rasped
As I gazed at her pink, silk, sleeveless dress with turquoise
    triskeles
And at her moist, fiery eyes rearing up in her skull.
"Ladies and gentlemen, our feature film tonight is *The Flamingo
    Kid*.
We'll be commencing our take-off in approximately five
    minutes."
As we continued to taxi she showed me her bottle of Drambuie –
"Duty-free!"
High over Kennedy, as we turned tail on Manhattan,
Heading out over Long Island for the North Atlantic,
She had a member of the cabin crew fetch her a baby scotch
And a tumbler chock-a-block with ice cubes.
She sighed: "I don't drink myself,"
As I stared down at the Cape Cod coastline,
"Except, of course, when I'm flying.
Rusty Nails is what I like – Drambuie and scotch."

I could not keep my eyes off her as she guzzled it down,
And the urban necklaces far below on the breast of the coastline.
"Do you know," she remarked, "you are a truly handsome
    little man.
I feel proud to be sitting beside you – with an empty seat
    between us."
Before I could begin to make my puny reply, she added:
"Cheer up – the worst that could happen would be if we
    crashed.
Imagine floating about in the midst of all this debris and
    wreckage."
I glanced around at my 350 fellow passengers,
All sunset and chains.
She disembarked at Shannon at dawn in the mist
And I flew on to Dublin, not worried whether I lived to tell the
    tale
Of how I had had the great good fortune
To fly from New York to Dublin with *The Flamingo Kid*
Clutching a glass of Rusty Nails in her freckled claws,
Her beaked eyes playing on the floodwaters of her smile:
"Cheer up – the worst that could happen would be if we
    crashed.
Imagine floating about in the midst of all this debris and
    wreckage."

A Vision of Africa on the Coast of Kerry

On the coast at Meenogahane,
Near Causeway,
Nellie presides in the kitchen of her cottage,
At eighty-five, exchanging the time of day
With tourists, educating us:
Nellie who has never in her life
Been out of her townland
Except "the wanst".
Five years ago at eighty,
When she had a stroke,
She was transported
By county ambulance
To the Regional Hospital in Cork.
Do you know what I saw there?
No, Nellie, what did you see?
I saw a black man.
A black man?
A black man — you should have seen his neck!
His neck?
Oh the neck of him — the lovely neck of him!
The lovely, wet, shiny, rubbery neck of him!
I asked him if he would let me put my hand on it
And he did, he let me —
And it was all black, do you know?
Oh it was lovely, I tell you, lovely!

Martha's Wall

Her pleasure – what gave her pleasure – was to be walked
Down her wall, the South Wall, a skinny, crinkly, golden-
    stemmed wall
That contracts and expands, worms and unworms, in and out of
    Dublin Bay,
Across the sea's thighs pillowing in, besotted, under daisy-
    gartered skies.
She'd curl her finger around my finger and I'd lead her out on
    to it.
She liked it when the flowering sea was shedding spray across it.
She'd tense up with delight to see me get wet
And wetter still, and wetter – the wetter it was
The better she liked it, and me – and she wanted always
To get down, away down, to the very end of it
Where there is a deep-red lighthouse, and the deep-red
    lighthouse
Was hers also, hers, and we'd sit down on a bench under it
And she'd put her arm around my neck and we'd stop needing
    to speak
And we'd sit there, breathless, in silence, for a long time.

Doris Fashions

to Sarah

On the instructions of the parole officer, I telephoned the prison
At 1 p.m. from the main post office in town.
They said they'd send a prison van in to collect me.
While I was waiting—I had to wait about an hour—
Leaning up against the post-office wall in the noonday sun
I caught a glimpse of myself in the display window
Of a shop across the street—Doris Fashions.
I glimpsed a strange man whom I do not know
And whom, when on the odd occasion I have glimpsed him
    before,
I have not warmed to—his over-intense visage,
Hurted, hurtful,
All that ice, and all that eyebrow.
I averted my eyes from the mirror-image in Doris Fashions,
Yet thinking that it is good that Doris Fashions—
That there is that much
To be salvaged from the wreckage of the moment—
That Doris Fashions.

If you had a daughter called Doris, and after you had spent
    years
Rearing her and schooling her and enjoying her and loving her,
She left home and set up shop in a country town
And called it Doris Fashions—how would you feel?
You would be proud of her, wouldn't you?
Or if you fell in love with a girl called Doris
And it turned out that she had a little shop of her own
Called Doris Fashions—you'd be tickled pink, wouldn't you?

All my life I've dreamed of having a motto of my own—

My own logo – my own signature tune.
Waiting for the prison van to collect me,
In the window of Doris Fashions I see into myself
And I adopt as my own logo, my own signature tune,
Doris Fashions –
Trying it out to myself on the road out to the prison:
Doris Fashions Paul Durcan – Paul Durcan Doris Fashions.
For who made the world?
Doris made the world –
And I believe in Doris, and in Doris only,
And never – never – never – never – never – never – never
In John O'Donoghue.

The Beckett at the Gate

to Derek Mahon

That spring in Dublin
You could not go anywhere
Without people barking at you,
Button-holing you in the street and barking at you,
Accosting you and barking at you:
"Have you not seen Barry McGovern's Beckett?"
Or else, which was worse,
"Have you not been to the Beckett at the Gate?"
I was fed up with people barking at me:
"Have you not seen Barry McGovern's Beckett?
Have you not been to the Beckett at the Gate?"

"No, I have not seen Barry McGovern's Beckett—
No, I have not been to the Beckett at the Gate—
I'd mutter, affecting
To look under my legs
As if it was I
Who was the weary, put-upon virtuoso of bathos,
My limp tail of ejection.
In any case, I am not mad
About going to the theatre,
Going alone to the theatre
Upon a gloomy night in May.
It was, therefore, in spite of myself,
Quite against the grain,
That I took the initiative
By booking a ticket
For a Tuesday night at the Gate
In the third week of May

For Barry McGovern's Beckett,
The Beckett at the Gate.
C9 was the number of my ticket,
Centre, third row from the front.
I got there in good time.
I like to get to a thing in good time
Whatever it is — the bus into town,
Or the bus back out of town —
With at least a quarter of an hour to spare,
Preferably half an hour, ample time
In which to work up an adequate steam of anxiety.
When I stepped into the auditorium
I was relieved to see it was near empty,
I was heartened to see
That it was near empty,
Four or five patrons
Scattered about the theatre.

Consoled, a little less disconcerted
By the general regatta,
A little less addled
By the whole regrettable adventure,
A little less regretful
That I had not stayed put
In my bedsit,
I made my way to my seat,
Only to discover that one
Of the four or five patrons
Scattered about the near-empty theatre
Transpired to be ensconced
In the adjacent tip-up seat
Right next to my own.
In silence we sat, side by side,
All the house-lights on,

For the entire fifteen minutes before curtain-up.
I felt a right, roaring idiot,
Crouched there in all that silence
In row C of the Gate
Shoulder to shoulder with that—
That other human being
A woman to boot,
A young woman to boot.

To make matters worse
She was more sprawled than seated,
More dispersed than disposed,
More horizontal than vertical,
Engrossed in a paperback book
The name of which by dint
Of craning of the neck
I did manage to pick out.
It was a Picador paperback
Entitled *One Hundred Years of Solitude.*
As if that was not bad enough
There was not enough leg-room;
So that I had to scrunch up my legs,
Thereby having to sit closer to her.
A minute before the performance began
Someone (obviously some kind of friend,
Some ilk of accomplice)
Hailed her from five rows back:
"Michelle, Michelle!"
I said to myself
If only Michelle's friends
Would invite Michelle to sit with them
Then I'd have all of row C
To myself which at least
Would make the next hour and a half

If not less of a cauchemar
At least a bearable cauchemar.
But no – Michelle stayed put
And the lights went out,
And the curtain up,
And I knew I was for it.
Why had I let myself
Be bothered and browbeaten
By all those cultural groupies
Going on, and on, and on,
"Have you not seen Barry McGovern's Beckett?
Have you not been to the Beckett at the Gate?"

Well, it was out of the top drawer,
As Joseph Holloway would have put it,
Or would not have put it.
Not since the Depression of the 1950s
And the clowns in Duffy's Circus
Have I laughed myself so sorry,
So sorry that I was ready to shout,
If anyone else had shouted:
"Stop Beckett! Stop McGovern!"

And Michelle? Well, Michelle –
I mean talk about Susannah,
Or Judith and Holofernes,
Or any or all of those females
In the Old Testament,
Sarah or Rachel or even Eve;
Not to mention the New Testament,
Martha or Mary or Magdalen –
Michelle was – well, Michelle.
All right, I ought to have said
She was exceptionally petite –

But it's a small point
And to dwell on it
Would detract from her own performance.
She gave herself over to her own laughter
To such an exuberant extent
That she was wholly inside it – within the orbit
Of her own transparent laughter,
All rouge and polythene.
Every time she laughed
She kicked me in the legs,
In the backs of my legs,
Or nudged me in the kneecaps –
Unintentionally, of course.
Abruptly, she sat up in her seat
Tucking her legs in under her bottom –
Crimson red booties, blue skin-tight jeans,
Airy black blouse.
She leaned her head on my shoulder,
As if we had been espoused for years,
Donkeys' years, camels' years, elephants' years.
Occasionally, at a particularly
Outrageous piece of malarkey
By Beckett-McGovern,
She'd grip my arm tight
And howl – luminously howl.
Well, obviously, things
Had got quite out of hand
And I wanted to say to her
"Please please please please
Go on doing what you're doing."
But I did not say anything.
A mum's-the-word man
Is what I am;
Not a word to the Reverend Mother,

Not a smoke-signal to Chief Sitting Mountain.
If there was an interval – and it said
In the programme that there was
An interval of fifteen minutes –
I do not remember any interval.
All I remember is Michelle's head
On my shoulder, and the kick
Of her hair brushing against my cheekbone.
Many years had elapsed since last
I had been made aware of my cheekbone –
Her mousy hair brushing against it,
Scented, and wet, and calamitous.

When the curtain came down
And the applause had drained away
I turned around to gaze
In rapture at Michelle
But she had slipped away.
Mother of God
Chosen by the Eternal Council!
I walked back down along O'Connell Street,
Muttering to myself,
"Have you not seen Barry McGovern's Beckett?
Have you not been to the Beckett at the Gate?"
Every few steps, covertly,
I gave a kick in the air:
"Have you not seen Barry McGovern's Beckett?
Have you not been to the Beckett at the Gate?"
It was dusk – lucid,
Warm, limpid,
On O'Connell Street Bridge.
Spilling over with self-pity
And lasciviously gazing down
At the bicycle-filled waters

Of the River Liffey running on, on,
I elected to walk on
Back to my bedsit in Ringsend
(Instead of taking the bus)
Through the East European parts of Dublin City,
Past the gasometer and Grand Canal Dock,
Misery Hill, The Gut, The Drain,
The Three Locks, Camden, Buckingham, Westmoreland.
At Ringsend there was a full moon over
The Sugar Loaf and the Wicklow Hills,
And the crimson lights of the telecommunications aerial
On the Three Rock Mountain were trembling
And on the television transmitter in Donnybrook;
And the hand-painted signs of the local public houses,
FitzHarris's and The Oarsman,
Looked childmade in the lamplight, homely
By the River Dodder,
As I balanced in a trance on the humpbacked bridge,
On a fulcrum of poignancy,
And I felt like a stranger in a new city,
An urchin in a New Jerusalem,
A bareheaded protagonist
In a vision of reality,
All caught up in a huge romance,
In a hot erotic cold tumult.
On the street corner in Ringsend village
Not at, but close to, a bus stop,
A tiny young woman was standing,
Hovering, twirling, stamping,
And when I saw that it was Michelle –
As I passed her by
She scrutinized me serenely
As if she had never seen me before –
As if she had never seen me before.

I keep on walking;
I'll go on, I think, I'll go on.
Next year in Carrickmines
I'll play tennis with whatever
Woman will play tennis with me
And I'll never be never again.
Next year in Carrickmines.
On grass. Love all.
Fifteen Love. Thirty Love. Forty Love.
Deuce. Advantage Miss Always.
Game, Set and Match.
Why you, Michelle? why you?
Will you join me? Join me?
If you're the joining kind, please join me.
Next year in Carrickmines,
Greystones, Delgany, Killiney, Bray, Dalkey, Shankill,
  Kilmacud,
Galloping Green, Stillorgan – perhaps even Dublin.

There's a beckett at the gate, there's a beckett
                at the gate, Michelle;
There's a Beckett at the gate, there's a Beckett
                at the gate, Michelle;
There's a beckett at the Gate, there's a beckett
                at the Gate, Michelle;
There's a Beckett at the Gate, there's a Beckett
                at the Gate, Michelle.

The Woman with the Keys to Stalin's House

You would imagine – would you not –
That the town of Gori,
The town of Joseph Vissarionovich Dzhugashvili,
By virtue of being just that –
Stalin's home town –
Would be a self-centred, uninhabited, pock-marked crater,
"The town that gave birth to . . ."

Galya has lived all her life in the town of Gori
Under the statue of Stalin,
A buxom, humorous, lugubrious woman,
Her ash-blond nail varnish matching her ash-blond hair
Corbelled in a ponytail.
After traipsing about the Stalin Museum
And the house where Stalin was born,
Which Stalin personally had preserved as a monument to
    himself –
Sentimental Soso –
We had a meal together in the local hotel
Around the corner in Stalin Square
"I am the saddest woman in all Georgia,"
She remarked to me with a smile
That played on her mauve-painted lips
Long after her words had died,
Spreadeagling her arms
So that her breasts could breathe
In the asphyxiating atmosphere,
Black rain knifing the windowpane.
While we ate and drank in silence

She opened the buttons of her blouse,
Beckoning me to follow suit.
She motioned to me to open my mouth
And swilling her own mouth with champagne,
She put her lips to mine,
Letting the champagne swill
Into my mouth from her mouth.
The mountains askew above the town
Leaned slightly across the sky
As we lurched around the room
Making big love and little love.
We bathèd one another
With jug and basin.
As I towelled her down
She shut her eyes, tightly.
Stalin Street was deserted
As we embraced goodbye.
She remarked:
"I like you a little because you have mixed feelings."
In the car returning to Tbilisi,
Riding down the Georgian Military Highway,
I considered that if Eve had been even half as affectionate
As Galya in Gori,
Well, how lucky I was to have been her Adam;
And Jahweh – that old Stalin on his plinth –
Had failed to cow us. Galya,
Can there be anyone in the world who has not got mixed
    feelings?
Should there be anyone in the world who has not got
    mixed feelings?

Trauma Junction

The answer to your question is that I am not your mother;
Your mother was another mother and she died in Russia.

Estonian Farewell, 1983

to Arvo

Midwinter in the snowed-up port of Tallinn,
Midnight on the platform of Tallinn railway station,
Leaning out the window of the midnight train
As it begins to pull out for Leningrad and fever,
And Arvo rooted to the platform waving farewell to us,
Clutching in his hands
A little book in blue-and-gold wrappers—
Teach Yourself Irish by Myles Dillon.

Arvo, I have been to the moon and found you;
I wave and you wave; you wave and I wave;
As you squat there in your furry nimbus,
And my mother—a ghost with a knife through her halo—
Is stumbling through the birch trees to keep up with the train,
The birch trees between the tracks and the fields,
And she is crying, crying, crying, crying, crying, crying:
"My son, my son, why hast thou forsaken me?"

Peredelkino: at the Grave of Pasternak

to A. K. Avelichev

After all these years, Boris Leonidovich Pasternak,
I have found you.
How self-engrossed and paranoid I must appear to you
Lurking at the foot of your grave,

A blue corduroy cap on my head
That I purchased in a West-of-Ireland village;
A green scarf tied around my throat,
A Japanese automatic camera in my hand.

But you are not vexed by my foibles –
If anything you rejoice in and applaud me –
A middle-aged gear-laden telephone engineer
Frantic to grapple with your trinity of pines.

Be still, my strapped-up and harnessed soul.
I begin at last to stand at ease.
Instead of grappling with them, I overhear myself
Conversing with the Father, the Son and the Holy Spirit.

But it is they who do most of the conversing.
I am amazed by their point of view.
Although the enemy once again is almost
At the gates of Moscow and Borodino,

They egg me to pay no heed:
Instead of darkening my energy
With bombast and humbug
I should daub my soul with leaves of mud.

While warplanes fly to and fro overhead
And cars race up and down the Kiev Highway,
Pay heed to the housewife on the skyline,
On whose head God has put a price.

At the heart of atheism God is at home;
Man locked into history opening the door.
Closer to God is the atheist opening the door
Than the churchman closing the door in your face.

II

Strange that anybody can visit your grave,
 Even a naïf like me;
Surely the dead are entitled to privacy,
 If not also the living.

Your grave out here in the Vineyard of Peredelkino
 Is open to all comers:
I gaze through the railings at your headstone,
 Let myself in by the gate.

I am borne back to another railing'd grave
 In Kilcrea in West Cork:
"Lo Arthur Leary, generous, handsome, brave,
 Slain in his bloom lies in this humble grave."

Slain in his bloom like you,
 Lo Boris Leonidovich;
Who died for the right to ride a white horse;
 You—generous, handsome, brave.

Sitting down on the wooden bench, I note
 That it is I who am trapped in life

Whilst in death you are free,
    Golden eagle on a black leaf.

Over the grave of Art O'Leary at midnight
    On a summer's evening,
Your young priest-like friend from Zima, Yevtushenko,
    Broke — broke a bottle of red wine.

Somewhere in the petals of the crowd in the metro
    My dead mother is peering out at me;
My mother who went to Russia when I was three
    And who died in Moscow.

Somewhere in the trees of the hand-painted forest
    Ivinskaya is peering out at me;
A man without his woman is a right hand without a left;
    I kiss the back of her wrought-bone hand.

Voices of a man and a woman through the foliage,
    A father and mother
At the fresh grave next to yours of a nineteen-year-old boy
    Slain in the Afghanistan wars.

I have not read the novel of *Doctor Zhivago*,
    Yet I lack the courage to say so;
Isn't it heartbreakingly funny how relentlessly
    Pretentious men are.

How often I myself have met intellectuals
    Who have read Bulgakov
They say — whose faces go blank if you talk
    To them about Titian Tabidze.

All alone at your grave, I have a two-hour conversation
    With myself and the trees;
My blue corduroy cap perched all alone
    On the damp bench watching us.

A babushka is propelling herself like a pram
    Across the road with three goats;
In the car returning to Moscow, the driver remarks
    "Your blue cap looks Jewish – is it German?"

That night we make love in an apartment beside
    The Cultural Palace of the Ball-Bearing Plant;
Next morning under Shevchenko's statue by the Moskva River
    I set fire to my cap.

Oh Song of the Blue Cap, for Boris Leonidovich,
    From the West of Ireland.
It makes a soft explosion (two books of matches inside it),
    An orgasm of gentleness.

In the leaf-strewn post-coital smoke-pall,
    The cars do not stop reiterating your name
As they race down Kalinin Prospekt to Red Square –
    Pasternak! Pasternak!

Moskviches, Zhigulis, Volgas, Chaikas,
    And the odd, conspicuous Zil:
Pasternak, Pasternak! Pasternak, Pasternak!
    Victory to the Blue Cap Boy.

Diarrhoea Attack at
Party Headquarters in Leningrad

An attack of diarrhoea at Party Headquarters in Leningrad
Was not something I imagined ever happening to me
Which is perhaps partly why it did happen to me.
The presidium had barely taken its place
Under the iconic portraits of V. I. Lenin and M. S. Gorbachev
When I could feel the initial missiles
Firing down the sky of my stomach
Setting in motion something that was irreversible –
The *realpolitik* of the irreversible.
The only consolation was that I was wearing underpants.
The fact is that sometimes I do not wear underpants.
Oddly enough I was wearing red underpants
Which I had originally purchased in Marks & Spencer's.
The first explosion resulted in immediate devastation –
The ensuing explosions serving only to define
The innately irreversible dialectic of catastrophe.
I whispered magnanimously into the earhole of my interpreter.
He reciprocated that since he also had "a trauma of the intestine"
We should both take our leave *immédiatement* and he showed me
Such fraternal solicitude that in my mind's eye
I can still see Lenin peering down at me
As if he were peering down at nobody else in the hall.
A black Volga whisked us back to our hotel and ignominy –
My ignominy – not anybody else's ignominy – and that night
Over cups of tea we discussed the war in Afghanistan,
Agreeing that realistically it appeared an insoluble problem,
Yet hoping against hope that somehow it would be solved
And that – as you put it, Slava – "Russian boys come home."
There is nothing necessarily ignominious about anything.

Tbilisi Cabaret
(Ortachala Belle with a Fan)

IN MEMORIAM N. PIROSMANI

I'm a sophisticated primitive.
I'm going bald but I don't chase
After my hair, and when I sway
My hips—it is for you.
Tell me you appreciate my authoritative wrists,
Tell me you savour the scent of my sweat,
And I will tell you on your fortieth birthday
That you're a girl at heart.

O my dear one, warm to me.
I will always warm to you.

I'm a sophisticated primitive.
It is you who is the prima donna
Forever much more prima and more donna
Than the man who likes to state—
The man who is not afraid to state—
That love is greater than God or Marx.
A woman's love made the world.
I believe in woman.

O my dear one, warm to me.
I will always warm to you.

I'm a sophisticated primitive.
I like to bring my own chair
To the party, and at the height

Of the party there is nowhere I like better
To sit than under the table nursing
A bottle of you, your smiling silence,
Until abruptly, after sixty-nine years,
You winkle me out and lick me.

O my dear one, warm to me.
I will always warm to you.

I am a citizen of a secret society.
Although God was born in Russia
It is a well-kept secret.
In Red Square on Palm Sunday
I looked through Brezhnev's eyes
When they were open, and I saw
Ten thousand secret faces wave up at me.
"Jesus, it's May Day!" he growled at me.

O my dear one, warm to me.
I will always warm to you.

Our Lady of Red Square, pray for us.
Midnight Trolleybus, pray for us.
Ice cream in Winter, pray for us.
Queen of the Moscow Metro, pray for us.
Leaf of Gold, pray for us.
Hammer and Sickle, pray for us.
Mother of Intercourse, pray for us.
Taxi at Dawn, pray for us.

Ortachala Belle, may to me on May Day.
On May Day may I always may to you.

Hymn to My Father

Dear Daddy, on your last legs now,
Can you hear me
In your bedroom in the treetops,
Chained to your footwarmer and your pills,
Death notices in newspapers your exclusive reading?
We had no life together – or almost none.
Yet you made me what I am –
A man in search of his Russia.
After schooldays I became a poet –
A metamorphosis you could no more fathom
Than I could fathom your own osmosis –
Lawyer with a secret life,
As secret as the life of a poet.
You had a history for every milestone,
A saga for every place name –
The Bovril Sign, the Ballast Office Clock, the Broadstone –
And so, at your knee, at your elbow, I became you.
Estranged as we are,
I am glad that it was in this life
I loved you,
Not the next.
O Russian Knight at the Crossroads!
If you turn to the right, you will lose your horse;
To the left, your head;
If you go straight on, your life.
If you were me – which you are –
Knight at the Crossroads,
You would go home to Russia this very night.

The Red Arrow

In the history of transport — is there any other history? —
The highest form of transport is the Red Arrow,
The night train from Leningrad to Moscow.
With whom will I be sharing my compartment tonight?
The editor of the *Jazz Front Gazette*, it transpires.
But, affable, polite, as she is, how can she compare
With Svetka with whom I shared in 1981?
We sat up half the night chin-wagging, colloguing,
And when awkwardly I began to undress and she said:
"Ah yes, it is all right — would you like to?"
Naturally I liked to,
And the train was about halfway between Leningrad and
    Moscow
When I fell out of her bunk on to the floor
And the wagon-lady put her head in the door
To check what was the matter
And Svetka said in Russian: "These foreigners
They cannot even keep from falling out of bed —
Always needing to be treated like babies."
The wagon-lady grunted and slid the door shut
And I climbed back into the bunk with Svetka.
Each time we made love she groaned:
"I am the little horse in your snow."
I let up the window blind and, as we made love again —
A blizzard upside down at the windowpane —
When she opened her eyes, she murmured
"You are snowing on my tail, my dear man."
As the Red Arrow flew into Moscow, Svetka said:
"My dear man, you must meet me tomorrow.

Tell them you have a problem with your business.
Meet me in the Melodiya Music Store on Kalinin.
I will be in the Classical Russian Music section.
Look me up under Rachmaninov."

It was a grey Moscow afternoon – not a bead of sunlight –
But we traipsed up and down the Arbat in seventh heaven.
"My dear, dear man," she keeps murmuring over and over.
Although that was all of seven years ago –
She who shot the Red Arrow through my heart.

Going Home to Russia

to A. Voznesensky

Hanging about the duty-free in Shannon Airport,
Waiting for the flight to Moscow to be called;
Waiting for the Havana–Moscow Illushin 62
To come in for refuelling, and to pick me up.

I am the solitary passenger joining the flight at Shannon;
The Irish immigration officer eyes me mournfully;
"Good luck," he mutters as if to say "you will need it";
He does not know that I am versed in luck.

"Good luck," he mutters as if to a hostage or convict,
Not knowing that he is speaking to an Irish dissident
Who knows that in Ireland scarcely anybody is free
To work or to have a home or to read or write.

We Irish have had our bellyful of *blat*
And *blarney*, more than our share
Of the *nomenklatura* of Church and Party,
The *nachalstvo* of the legal and medical mafia.

Going down the airbridge, I slow my step,
Savouring the moment of liberation;
As soon as I step aboard the Aeroflot airliner
I will have stepped from godlessness into faith:

Into a winter of shoe-swapping;
Into a springtime of prams;
Into a summer of riverbanks and mountain huts;
Into an autumn of mushroom-hunting.

It is not until I am aboard the carrier
That I realise I am going home;
I have been ill at ease – on tenterhooks –
Because I have not realised I am going home.

Yet the doorway of the aircraft is still open;
The airbridge has not yet been disconnected;
At the last moment I might be taken off –
Not until we are airborne will I be free.

At the entrance to the cabin the pilot looms,
Shirtsleeves rolled up to his elbows;
He has the look of the long-distance bus driver
On the Galway–Limerick–Cork route:

A man much loved by his wife and friends;
The shape of his mind is the shape of the route;
Smoking his Cosmos, what is he thinking of?
He knows every bend in the road, every skyline,

And that the world, despite obstinate man, is round.
He will bend over the Baltic;
He will turn a corner at Riga, and at Moscow
He will let Asia run her fingers through our hair.

Take-off – the hips of the Shannon Estuary;
The pores of the gooseflesh of Ireland;
Wet, unrequited yearnings by the prickly inch;
The River Shannon lying crumpled on the mudflats of Foynes.

Copenhagen – the Baltic – Riga – Smolensk –
If there be a heaven, then this is what
It must feel like to be going down into heaven –
To be going home to Russia.

Beyond Smolensk the long approach begins,
The long approach into Moscow;
From far out at an angle of forty-five degrees,
The long descent into Sheremetyeva.

By his engine-murmurs, the pilot sounds like a man
Who has chosen to make love instead of to rape;
He caresses the Russian plains
With a long, slow descent — a prolonged kiss.

With the night down below us, with Russia
Under her mantle of snow and forest;
A block of flats lights up out of nowhere —
The shock in a lover's eyes at the impact of ecstasy.

O Svetka, Svetka! Don't, don't!
Say my name, Oh say my name!
O God O Russia! Don't, don't!
Say my name, Oh say my name!

In the aftermath of touchdown, gently we taxi;
We do not immediately put on our clothes;
In the jubilation of silence we taste our arrival —
The survival of sex.

The nose of the jet interlocks with the doorway;
At the top of the airbridge a militiaman stands smiling;
Outside the arrivals building I get lost in the snow;
I meet a woman who is also lost in the snow.

Going home to Russia to be with you —
Dark secret of life;
Going home to Russia to be with you —
Svetka in the snow.

Block after block after block after block—
You are squeaky-sick with laughter that I've come home;
Your neighbour, Madame Noses, sneaks a peep at me—
Dear, dear Svetka.

For sure I have no TV, and my radio
I use only for these weather reports:
This way we do it—it is good, no?
There are so many of us, so many.

I have come home to you to greet you
To watch with you the trains for Yaroslavl;
Train after train from your fifth-storey window—
What contentment! It is Moscow, and we are alone.

I have come home to you to greet you
In your own tiny kitchen—a kitchen lit for lovers;
To press red maple leaves between the pages of books,
To take off my tin hat and put on your shoes;

To sleep with you on the settee and to become with you
Creatures of the new forest, crushed deer;
Never again to have to endure the persecution
Of landlords, the humiliation of advertisers;

To live again with nature as before I lived
In Ireland before all the trees were felled;
Bouquets of leaves in Moscow in October,
Closer to you than I am to myself.

My dear loved one, let me lick your nose;
Nine months in your belly, I can smell your soul;
Your two heads are smiling—not one but both of them—
Isn't it good, Svetka, good, that I have come home?

O Svetka, Svetka! Don't, don't!
Say my name, Oh say my name!
O God O Russia! Don't, don't!
Say my name, Oh say my name.

1986

Putney Garage

to Brian Fallon

The morning after the poetry reading
At the Poetry Society in Earl's Court Square
I decided to go to a film in Leicester Square,
Having already that auburn October day
Changed my mind five times.
I would catch the 4.35 p.m. showing
Of *Au Revoir Les Enfants* in the Première.
I strolled along the north side of Piccadilly
But the closer I came to the cinema
The more I felt like going home to Brixton,
To Bill and Pippa, Ben and Sam and Jo,
In 64 Milton Road,
Pampas grass in the front garden,
Up the lane from Electric Avenue,
The child's playground that is London in October,
Its wild mildness, its puberty,
Kick of spentoutedness in my calf muscles.

I crossed over to the south side of Piccadilly,
Retraced my steps.
At the bus stop outside the Egyptian State Tourist Office
Francis Bacon was waiting for a bus;
Those ancient, glittering eyes on black steel rods
Socketed in their Sicilian pouches;
That teenager's ageing mouth
All cheek and tongue-in-cheek.

I fell into line.
We stood in silence,

He lounging against the corner of the bus shelter
In a lounge suit,
Hands in trench-coat pockets,
Belted trench coat flapping open, loose, horny epaulettes,
Black polished shoes, one over t'other,
Idly alert,
Courtly corner boy.

Luckily I had not got with me my pocket Olympus camera.
Two number 19s passed,
Flocks of cabs.
I did not allow advertisements for the pyramids
And for a boy Pharaoh
To distract me from the nape of Bacon's neck,
The henna-dyed hairs, gelled, spiky,
Gilded in October evening sun.
The breeze lifted the hair on the crown of his skull,
The proud, soft, blown comb of the cock.

A number 14 bus sailed into view,
The Statue of Eros in its rearview mirror.
He put out his hand,
His left hand – bare, ungloved.
He stepped up onto the platform.
But although he was first in the queue
He stood back to permit
A young Asian gentleman,
Lean, prematurely grey,
To cut inside him to the lower deck.
Then he, aged eighty years,
Swung up the staircase like a gibbon
In the Dublin zoo.

I stepped back out of the queue,
Mulling on Vincent's memorial in Auvers
By Osip Zadkine – man at work or
Study of a man in a landscape.
I studied him sit himself down
Halfway down the aisle of the upper deck
On the north side.
What to call it? And by whom?
"Good Evening, Childhood" by J. M. W. Turner?
The bus sailed out into the smog-scrapered sun
Towards Hyde Park and Kensington,
Its terminus in white on black:
Putney Garage.

Hommage à Cézanne

This morning when I am trying to get myself
   together for work,
Piece myself together for work,
Shaving with one hand and making coffee with the
   other,
There's a ring on the door bell and it's Olympia:
"There's a horse on my staircase, Paul."
I am forty-three – Olympia is nineteen.
She stands there laconically
In a miniskirt the size of a hanky
And a black bowler hat and a white blouse
And a green suede hunting jacket:
"There's a horse on my staircase, Paul."

I do not know what I am supposed to do about it.
I procrastinate on the balls of my feet,
Trying to wipe the shaving cream from off my face
And glancing down at the span-new coffee stain
On my turquoise cotton shirt.
She gives me the sort of cat-on-the-wall smile
That twangs its garters between tail-swishes:
"You and I have a secret
But neither of us knows what it is."

I do not know what it is.
Foggily, I do not know what it is.
Then she says that thing to me again:
"There's a horse on my staircase, Paul,"
And just as I am about to say to her "Come in,"

She steps up to me on the tips of her toes
And flicks me a kiss high on the cheekbone
And spins around and steps back into the elevator.
I step back into my apartment
And squirt some shaving cream into my coffee filter
And stir my mug with my razor:
"There's a horse on my staircase, Paul."

I am walking around in circles in my own apartment.
I am supposed to be at work one hour ago.
What am I supposed to say to my boss?
My boss is a chic fifty-seven-year-old mother of five:
"Paul, why don't you go to sleep for a week?
We can take a look at your equestrian needs
When you get to feeling a little less distracted."

Am I dreaming?
No, I am not dreaming.
I can hear the sound of my own hooves
Stamping on the marble steps of her staircase.
I go back to sleep again
To the sound of my own hooves
Stamping on the marble steps of her staircase:
"You are the horse on my staircase, Paul."

The Barrie Cooke Show, May 1988

After the Barrie Cooke show,
Although I had no money,
I took a taxi
Back to my room in Ringsend.

With no money in my pockets
I flew in a Mercedes Benz
Back to my room in Ringsend.
From the back seat of the taxi—
Blue Cabs No. 1379—
I gave my blessing to the world,
To the left of me,
To the right of me.

After I'd borrowed the fare off a neighbour
And waved goodbye to the taxi driver
I stripped.
I stretched out on the bed
And I opened the window—
My window with the broken sash
Propped up by the jar of Vaseline
Put there by the previous tenant,
The lady who died of cancer—
And I let in the wind and the sun
And I switched on the telly
And I watched the end of a one-day
County cricket match in Essex:
Seven runs to win
And five balls to bowl.

Naked I lay face down on the bed
With my head propped up in my left hand
While I looked back over my right shoulder at the telly.
My legs were spreadeagled on the duvet
And I could feel the breeze at the base of my spine
And on the foot of my coccyx.
When you touched me there once with your forefinger
I stepped off a plane in mid-air.

Seven runs to win
And five balls to bowl.
When you touched me there once with your forefinger
I stepped off a plane in mid-air.

Loosestrife in Ballyferriter

to Brian Friel on his sixtieth birthday

I

Dear Master – Homesick for Athens
In this summer of rain, I prayed to the Mother
Of God but she did not appear to answer
And the Loosestrife in Ballyferriter near broke my heart.

II

But then I came to the Gallarus Oratory.
Its small black door-space was a Mount of Venus.
Within the womb of that miniature iconostasis
What I saw was a haven white as salt.

III

An Trá Bhán, an Trá Bhán,
Cá bhfuil m'athair, cá bhfuil mo mháthair?
An Trá Bhán, an Trá Bhán,
Cá bhfuil m'athair, cá bhfuil mo mháthair?

IV

I stood in the delivery ward outside the Gallarus Oratory,
Overtaken by coachload after coachload of tourists
From Celtic, from Medieval, from Modern times,
Expiring, only to be given birth to, in that small black
   door-space.

V

The embryonic majority were from the heel of Italy.
There were French, Swedish, German, Dutch.
There were siblings also from North America
To whom Ireland is an odyssey odder than Iowa.

VI

("Iowa" – she keened from behind a drystone wall –
"Iowa – I don't want to have to go to Iowa.
Iowa doesn't want me and I don't want Iowa.
Why must I forsake Ireland for Iowa?")

VII

There was a traffic snarl-up at the Gallarus Oratory,
All of the newly born vying to find parking space
In a gauntlet of fuchsia. In the small black door-space
I gave vent to my grief for my foreign mother.

VIII

What is the nature of Loosestrife in Ballyferriter?
What class of a massacre occurred on the Great Blasket?
Who burned the islanders out of their island homes?
Was it the Irish who burned us out of our island homes?

IX

What we did not know as we scurried out over the waves
In the rain-laden sunlight to feed our eyes on the corpse of the
    Blasket
Was that we were being observed from a small black door-space
By a small old man blacker than his own door-space.

X

Only the small old man living alone in his own black door-space,
Counting us swooping in and out of the corpse of the Blasket,
In the showdown saluted me and he whistled in the cosmos,
His eyes floating in the sheep's carcass of his skull,

XI

His larynx thinned by the white sand of his eyes:
"It was the Irish who burned us out of our island homes,"
And his smile was moist so that it stuck on the breeze:
"It was the Irish who burned us out of our island homes."

XII

An Trá Bhán, an Trá Bhán,
Cá bhfuil m'athair, cá bhfuil mo mháthair?
An Trá Bhán, an Trá Bhán,
Cá bhfuil m'athair, cá bhfuil mo mháthair?

XIII

Dear Master – Homesick for Athens
In this summer of rain, my closest grief
Lies in Tyrone dust. There is no man
Who would not murder his brother. Joy of all who grieve.

XIV

There is no God – only his Mother;
There is no God – only his Mother and;
There is no God – only his Mother and Loosestrife;
There is no God – only his Mother and Loosestrife in
    Ballyferriter.

Self-Portrait, Nude with Steering Wheel

I am forty-five and do not
Know how to drive a car
– And you tell me I am cultured.

Forty-five years creeping and crawling about the earth,
Going up and down the world,
And I do not know the difference between a carburettor and a
    gasket
– And you tell me I am a Homo sapiens.

Forty-five years sitting in the back seat giving directions
– And you say that I am not an egotist.

Forty-five years sitting in the passenger seat
With my gloved hands folded primly in my lap
– And you think I am liberated.

Forty-five years getting in and out of cars
And I do not know where the dipstick is
– And you tell me that I am a superb lover.

Forty-five years grovelling behind a windscreen
– And you talk of my pride and courage and self-reliance.

Forty-five years of not caring to know the meaning of words
Like transmission, clutch, choke, battery, leads
– And you say that I am articulate.

Forty-five years bumming lifts off other people –
And you tell me I am an independent, solitary, romantic spirit.

So it is that you find me tonight
Loitering here outside your front door
Having paid off a taxi in three ten-pound notes,
Nude, with a steering wheel in my hands.

The Centre of the Universe

Pushing my trolley about in the supermarket,
I am the centre of the universe;
Up and down the aisles of beans and juices,
I am the centre of the universe;
It does not matter that I live alone;
It does not matter that I am a jilted lover;
It does not matter that I am a misfit in my job;
I am the centre of the universe.

I'm always here, if you want me —
I am the centre of the universe.

I enjoy being the centre of the universe.
It is not easy being the centre of the universe
But I enjoy it.
I take pleasure in,
I delight in,
Being the centre of the universe.
At six o'clock a.m. this morning I had a phone call;
It was from a friend, a man in Los Angeles:
"Paul, I don't know what time it is in Dublin
But I simply had to call you:
I cannot stand LA so I thought I'd call you."
I calmed him down as best I could.

I'm always here, if you want me —
I am the centre of the universe.

I had barely put the phone down when it rang again,
This time from a friend in São Paulo in Brazil:
"Paul – do you know what is the population of São Paulo?
I will tell you: it is twelve million skulls.
Twelve million pairs of feet in the one footbath.
Twelve million pairs of eyes in the one fishbowl.
It is unspeakable, I tell you, unspeakable.
I calmed him down as best I could.

I'm always here, if you want me –
I am the centre of the universe.

IV

But then when the phone rang a third time and it was not yet
  6.30 a.m.,
The petals of my own hysteria began to awaken and unfurl.
This time it was a woman I know in New York City:
"Paul – New York City is a Cage,"
And she began to cry a little bit over the phone,
To sob over the phone,
And from three thousand miles away I mopped up her tears,
I dabbed each tear from her cheek
With just a word or two or three from my calm voice.

I'm always here, if you want me –
I am the centre of the universe.

V

But now tonight it is myself;
Sitting at my aluminium double-glazed window in Dublin City;

Crying just a little bit into my black T-shirt.
If only there was just one human being out there
With whom I could make a home? Share a home?
Just one creature out there in the night —
Is there not just one creature out there in the night?
In Helsinki, perhaps? Or in Reykjavik?
Or in Chapelizod? Or in Malahide?
So you see, I have to calm myself down also
If I am to remain the centre of the universe;
It's by no means an exclusively self-centred automatic thing
Being the centre of the universe.

I'm always here, if you want me —
I am the centre of the universe.

Paul

In the rush-hour traffic outside the centre-city church
I stood with my bicycle waiting for the lights to change –
A Raleigh bicycle with upright handlebars
That I had purchased for two pounds fifty pence in The Pearl –
When a priest in black soutane and white surplice
Materialized in the darkness of the porch.
He glided over to me:
"I am about to begin a funeral Mass but I have no mourners.
Would you be prepared to act as a mourner for me?"

As we paced up the aisle, the priest enlightened me:
"He was about the same age as yourself,
All we know about him is that his name was Paul."

I knelt in the front pew,
The coffin on trestles alongside me,
Its flat abdomen next to my skull.
I felt as a mother must feel
All alone in the maternity ward
With her infant in the cot at the foot of the bed,
A feeling that everything is going to be all right
But that we are all aliens in the cupboard,
All coat hangers in the universe.

The priest – a seven-foot-tall, silver-haired peasant in his
    eighties –
Instructed me to put my bicycle in the hearse beside the coffin.
He and I sat in front with the driver.
At a major traffic junction near the cemetery of Mount Prospect

We had to brake to avoid knocking down a small boy.
The car behind us bumped into our rear bumper,
Inducing the bicycle to bump against the coffin.
We recognised a prominent politician in the back seat blessing
   herself.
At the graveside as the priest said prayers
I got the feeling that the coffin was empty;
That Paul, whoever he was,
Was somewhere else.

"How do you know that his name was Paul?"
I asked the priest as we tiptoed away.
He handed me a creased sheet
Of blue vellum, unlined notepaper – Belvedere Bond:
Dear Paul – Thank you for your marriage proposal
But I am engaged to be married in Rome in June.
Best wishes always, Mary

Queen of Loneliness.

Phyllis Goldberg

Of all the women working in our office
Phyllis Goldberg is the quiestest, most polite, most solicitous,
Most diligent, most discreet, most generous.
She'd been with us about twenty years when she went sick
And George Webb asked me to drop in on her on the way
     home.
An old lady in a walking frame answered the door,
Motioned me upstairs with her eyebrows.
She was sitting up in bed naked
With a bottle of whiskey in one hand
And a half-pint tooth mug in the other.
I enquired:
"Is there anything I can do for you?"
She gazed upon me with tears in her eyes,
Owls of tears.
She blinked: "Make love to me,"
In a tone at once passionate and dispassionate.
Since boyhood I had dreamed of being seduced
By a woman in her bedroom –
Is there a man who has not? –
Yet now it was the last thing I wanted to do
Or have done to me.
I undressed,
Unbuttoning my crisp pink shirt over thin, hairy, white legs.

After we had made love –
Angry flesh –
She fell asleep
And I sat up in bed with her head in my lap,

Patting her damp brown hair.
As I came down the staircase
I felt like a minor French count
In a nineteenth-century film
After having strangled his mistress,
Putting on his top hat and white kid gloves,
Twirling his ivory-knobbed cane.
Her mother watched from her walking frame
As I crossed the hall floor to the door.
When I opened the door I was afraid to look back
In case I should find the walking frame empty.
As I picked my steps through the snow
All I could hear was an empty walking frame.
I began to hurry through the snow
For fear that the empty walking frame
Would begin to chase after me.
No one will ever believe me
That I did what I did
Because it seemed what I ought to do.

That night Phyllis Goldberg telephoned me,
The first and only time that she telephoned me in twenty years.
"Thank you for making love to me," she said.
"Not at all," I said,
"Glad to be –"
She put down the phone
And I sat down behind my desk in the dark,
At my silent word processor, with its chin in its hands,
And I waited.
I knew that it was only a matter of time
Before the door would open of its own accord
And in the half-light from the hallway
I would behold the shadow of the empty walking frame.
I would cry out for help but it would be too late.

The next day a card from Phyllis Goldberg would swoop
  through my letter box
With such a flutter that everybody in the cinema would behold
Its butterfly trajectory:
"Thank you for making love to me. Love. Phyllis Goldberg."

Felicity in Turin

We met in the Valentino in Turin
And travelled down through Italy by train,
Sleeping together.
I do not mean having sex.
I mean sleeping together.
Of which sexuality is,
And is not, a part.
It is this sleeping together
That is sacred to me.
This yawning together.
You can have sex with anyone
But with whom can you sleep?

I hate you
Because having slept with me
You left me.

The Dream of Life

A woman waiting for her man
In Dowth of the slow-footed consonants
Draws down the sash window of her bedroom.
A pair of house martins – the last house martins of summer –
From mud huts under eaves
Alight on the precipice
Of the top ledge of the window frame,
Testing their propellers, whirring,
The voyage to Africa,
Hawks in the cliffs of Sicily
Avid for food for their hawk chicks.

Ulysses

I am hiding from my father
On the roof of Joyce's Tower
In Sandycove.
He is downstairs in the gloom
Of the Joyce Museum
Exchanging euphemisms with the curator,
The poet Michael Hartnett,
Meteorological euphemisms,
Wet and cold for June.

I am standing at the battlements.
I am eighteen years old.
The battle is whether or not
He will buy a copy of *Ulysses*.
It is a battle about money
But it is a battle also about morality
Or "morals" as it is called.
It began this morning at the breakfast table
When I asked him for twenty-one shillings
To buy a copy of *Ulysses*.
He refused on the grounds that on top
Of it being an outrageous sum of money
Which a poorly paid judge could ill afford,
It was a notoriously immoral book.
Even the most liberal-minded Jesuits
Had condemned *Ulysses*
As being blasphemous as well as pornographic.
My mother jumped around from the kitchen sink:
"Give him the money for the wretched book

And let the pair of you stop this nonsense
For pity's sake.
Will we ever see peace and sense in this house?"
My father stormed out of the kitchen,
The *Irish Independent* under his arm:
"I'll not be party to subsidising that blackguard
Bringing works of blasphemy into this house.
In the year of Our Lord nineteen hundred and sixty-three
I will not be an accessory to blasphemy."

I caught the 46A bus out to Joyce's Tower,
Newly opened as a museum.
The curator offered to share with me
A carafe of vodka left over
From a literary soirée of the night before.
It was the day after Bloomsday.
Monday, 17 June 1963.
We sat in a compatible silence,
Contemplatively, affably,
Until upheaval of gravel
Eradicated reverie.
I rushed to the door and glimpsed
My father at the foot of the iron steps.
I climbed up to the roof, hoping to hide
From him up there in the marine fog,
Foghorns bleating in the bay.

I hear footsteps behind me, I know it is he.
He declares: "I suppose we will have to buy that book.
What did you say the name of it is?"
I tell him that the name of it is *Ulysses*.
I follow him down the staircase and he submits:
"Mr Hartnett, I understand
You stock copies of a book entitled *Ulysses*.

I would like to purchase one copy of same."
"Certainly, Your Lordship, certainly,"
Replies the ever-courteous, Chinese-eyed curator.
When from his wingbacked chair behind his desk
He takes from a drawer
A copy of the jade-jacketed *Ulysses*,
The Bodley Head edition,
My father asks him if he would have brown paper
With which to wrap the green, satanic novel,
Make a parcel out of it.
The curator peers into a wastepaper basket
"Made by the Blind",
As if peering down into a bottomless lift shaft,
Casts a funicular, questing second glance at my father
Before fishing out crumpled bags of brown paper
Which the night before had ferried bottles of vodka.
He lays them out on the desk top
And smoothes them, taking pains
To be obsequiously
Extra punctilious, extra fastidious.
Formally, he hands it over to my father,
As if delivering to some abstract and intractable potentate
A peace gift of a pair of old shoes.
My father pronounces: "Thank you, Mr Hartnett."
The curator, at his most extravagantly unctuous, replies:
"Very glad to be able to oblige you, Your Lordship."

My father departed Joyce's Tower with the book.
The next day when I asked my mother if she'd seen it
She said it was in their bedroom beside my father's bed.
Her bed was beside the window and his bed
Was between her bed and the wall.
There it was, on his bedside table,
Ulysses,

With a bookmarker in it – a fruitgum wrapper –
At the close of the opening episode.
When a few weeks later
I got to reading *Ulysses* myself
I found it as strange as my father
And as discordant.
It was not until four years later
When a musical friend
Gave me my first lessons
That *Ulysses* began to sing for me
And I began to sing for my father:
Daddy, Daddy,
My little man, I adore you.

Study of a Figure in a Landscape, 1952

AFTER FRANCIS BACON

— Did your bowels move today?
— Yes, Daddy.
— At what time did your bowels move today?
— At eight o'clock, Daddy.
— Are you sure?
— Yes, Daddy.
— Are you sure that your bowels moved today?
— I am, Daddy.
— Were you sitting down in the long grass?
— I was, Daddy.
— Are you telling me the truth?
— I am, Daddy.
— Are you sure you are not telling a lie?
— I am, Daddy.
— You are sure that your bowels moved today?
— I am, Daddy, but please don't beat me, Daddy.
  Don't be vexed with me, Daddy.
  I am not absolutely sure, Daddy.
— Why are you not absolutely sure?
— I don't know, Daddy.
— What do you mean you don't know?
— I don't know what bowels are, Daddy.
— What do you think bowels are?
— I think bowels are wheels, Daddy,
  Black wheels under my tummy, Daddy.
— Did your black wheels move today?
— They did, Daddy.
— Then your bowels definitely did move today.
— Yes, Daddy.

– You should be proud of yourself.
– Yes, Daddy.
– Are you proud of yourself?
– Yes, Daddy.
– Constipation is the curse of Cain.
– Yes, Daddy.
– You will cut and reap the corn today.
– Yes, Daddy.
– Every day be sure that your bowels move.
– Yes, Daddy.
– If your bowels do not move, you are doomed.
– Yes, Daddy.
– Are you all right?
– No, Daddy.
– What in the name of the Mother of God
  And the dead generations is the matter with you?
– I want to go to the toilet, Daddy.
– Don't just stand there, run for it.
– Yes, Daddy.
– Are you in your starting blocks?
– Yes, Daddy.
– When I count to three, leap from your starting blocks.
– I can't Daddy.
– Can't can't.
– Don't, Daddy, don't, Daddy, don't, Daddy, don't.

The One-Armed Crucifixion

AFTER GIACOMO MANZÙ

How many thousands of hours on the shore at Galway,
In the drizzle off the back of the sea,
On the sodden sands,
Did we spend hurling together, father and son?
Pucking the *sliotar*, one to the other,
Hour in, hour out, year in, year out.
How many thousands of times, old man,
Did you strike a high ball for your young son
To crouch, to dart, to leap,
To pluck the ball one-handed out of the climbing air?

Fjord

You were Abraham but you were also Jesus.
In your Jesus suit
You liked to teach for the sake of teaching.
You were a teacher before you were a judge.

You'd descend with a word like "fjord",
By the light of the standard lamp
On a winter's night in firelight,
Savour it, bless it, deposit it on my tongue.

"*Fjord*" – you'd announce – "is a Norwegian word."
I'd gaze up at your icicle-compacted face
As if you'd invented Norway and the Norwegian language
Especially for me.

You'd confide that we had fjords of our own in Ireland
And the noblest of all our fjords was in County Mayo,
The Killary fjord in the safe waters of whose deep, dark thighs
German submarines had lain sheltering in the war.

Look into your Irish heart, you will find a German U-boat,
A periscope in the rain and a swastika in the sky.
You were no more neutral, Daddy, than Ireland was,
Proud and defiant to boast of the safe fjord.

Crinkle, near Birr

Daddy and I were lovers
From the beginning, and when I was six
We got married in the church of Crinkle, near Birr.
The *Irish Independent* photographed the wedding.
My mother gave me away.
My sister was best man.
He was forty-two and a TV personality in Yorkshire,
Close to his widowed mother in Mayo,
Always having his photograph taken,
Always grinning and polite and manly and coy and brittle,
Checking the stubs of his cheque books,
Tying up his used cheque books in elastic bands,
Putting money away for a rainy day,
Making gilt-edged investments.
It was in the days before he became a judge.
He compèred boxing fights and women's beauty contests
In an accent that was neither English nor Irish nor American.
It was known as the Athlone accent.
When he spoke of Athlone
Listeners were meant to think
Of a convent in the middle of a dark forest
To which the speaker was chaplain.

We went on our honeymoon
To Galway, the City of the Tribes.
We stayed in the Eglinton Hotel in Salthill.
For breakfast we ate grapefruit segments and toast
And the manager bowed, the waiters goosing around us.
We stood on the Salmon Bridge counting

Squadrons of salmon floating face down in the waters below,
Waiting to go upstream to spawn.

In the afternoons we spawned our own selves in our hotel
   bedroom
Listening to cricket.
The West Indies were playing the MCC at Lord's.
We lay in bed listening to Rohan Kanhai batting for a double
   century
And Garfield Sobers taking six wickets for forty-five runs.
O Owen of the Birds,
That is what it meant to be Irish and free –
To be father and son in bed together
In a hotel in the City of the Tribes
Listening to cricket on the BBC Radio Third Service.
After dinner we walked on the pier at Spiddal,
Holding hands, watching schools
Of porpoises playing in the apple-light of the western sea.
One night after dinner we drove to Gort,
Where Daddy let his hair down
And we played a game of cricket
In the back garden of another father-and-son couple.
When Daddy bowled, I was his wicketkeeper.
He fancied himself as Ray Lindwall
And I fancied myself as Godfrey Evans –
Godders jack-knifing over bails and stumps.
When we returned to the hotel, we entered
By the fire escape, feeling in a mood to be secretive,
Black iron staircase flicked up against white pebble-dash gable.
Daddy divided the human race
Into those who had fire escapes and spoke Irish
And those who had not got fire escapes and did not speak Irish.
Another night we sat in a kitchen in Furbo
With a schoolteacher hobnobbing in Irish

Exotic as Urdu, all that rain and night at the windowpane.

The marriage lasted five years.
On a summer's night in Newcastle West
After a game of cricket with boys my own age
I came back into the house without my school blazer.
"Where have you left your school blazer
Which you should not have been wearing in the first place?
School blazers are not for wearing.
School blazers cost money."
I had left it on a fence in the field.
When I went to retrieve it, it was lolling out of a cow's mouth,
One arm of it.
Daddy took off his trousers' belt,
Rolled it up in a ball round his fist,
And let fly at me with it.
In a dust storm of tears I glimpsed
His Western movie hero's eyes stare at me.

When I was twelve, I obtained a silent divorce.
Ireland is one of the few civilised countries —
And the only country outside Asia —
In this respect, that while husbands and wives
Can only at best separate,
Children can obtain a silent divorce from their parents.
When I look back at the years of my marriage to Daddy
What I remember most
Are not the beatings-up and the temper tantrums
But the quality of his silence when he was happy.
Walking at evening with him down at the river,
I lay on my back in the waters of his silence,
The silence of a diffident, chivalrous bridegroom,
And he carried me in his two hands home to bed.

Life-Saving

AFTER FRANCIS BACON

Having served my apprenticeship in tree climbing in Mayo,
I climbed up onto the roof of our Dublin home
By the banks of the Grand Canal
And knelt down at the skylight over your bedroom,
Feeding my nose into its pane of clear glass.
I could see you but not hear you.
Mother was reclining on her back on the carpet,
Kicking her legs in the air.
You dived between her knees,
Snaked your hands under her back,
Put down your head into her shoulder
And she locked her arms around your neck.
I could see her laughing with her eyes closed.
Not since the night of my twelfth birthday,
When she permitted me to take her
To the film of *War and Peace*
In the Adelphi in Middle Abbey Street,
Henry Fonda as Pierre,
Audrey Hepburn as Natasha,
Had I seen her look so inconsolably delighted – that anarchic
     smile
Of hers, so characteristic of her clan,
The MacBride clan
Of Antrim and Mayo.
Between the chimneypots
A barge was sliding past.
Back down in the kitchen after tea,
Offhandedly, I asked you what you'd been doing.
You replied without looking up from the table,

A chord of peremptory surrender in your voice:
"Your mother was teaching me life-saving.

Sport

There were not many fields
In which you had hopes for me
But sport was one of them.
On my twenty-first birthday
I was selected to play
For Grangegorman Mental Hospital
In an away game
Against Mullingar Mental Hospital.
I was a patient
In B Wing.
You drove all the way down,
Fifty miles,
To Mullingar to stand
On the sidelines and observe me.

I was fearful I would let down
Not only my team but you.
It was Gaelic football.
I was selected as goalkeeper.
There were big country men
On the Mullingar Mental Hospital team,
Men with gapped teeth, red faces,
Oily, frizzy hair, bushy eyebrows.
Their full forward line
Were over six foot tall
Fifteen stone in weight.
All three of them, I was informed,
Cases of schizophrenia.

There was a rumour
That their centre-half forward
Was an alcoholic solicitor
Who, in a lounge bar misunderstanding,
Had castrated his best friend
But that he had no memory of it.
He had meant well – it was said.
His best friend had had to emigrate
To Nigeria.

To my surprise,
I did not flinch in the goals.
I made three or four spectacular saves,
Diving full stretch to turn
A certain goal around the corner,
Leaping high to tip another certain goal
Over the bar for a point.
It was my knowing
That you were standing on the sideline
That gave me the necessary motivation –
That will to die
That is as essential to sportsmen as to artists.
More than anybody it was you
I wanted to mesmerise, and after the game –
Grangegorman Mental Hospital
Having defeated Mullingar Mental Hospital
By 14 goals and 38 points to 3 goals and 10 points –
Sniffing your approval, you shook hands with me.
"Well played, son."

I may not have been mesmeric
But I had not been mediocre.
In your eyes I had achieved something at last.
On my twenty-first birthday I had played on a winning team

The Grangegorman Mental Hospital team.
Seldom if ever again in your eyes
Was I to rise to these heights.

The Mayo Accent

Have you ever tuned in to the voice of a Mayoman?
In his mouth the English language is sphagnum moss
Under the bare braceleted feet of a pirate queen:
Syllables are blooms of tentativeness in bog cotton;
Words are bog oak sunk in understatement;
Phrases are bog water in which syllables float
Or in which speakers themselves are found floating face
   upwards
Or downwards;
Conversations are smudges of bogland under cloudy skies.
Speech in Mayo is a turbary function
To be exercised as a turbary right
With turbary responsibilities
And turbary irresponsibilities.
Peat smoke of silence unfurls over turf fires of language.

A man with a Mayo accent is a stag at bay
Upon a bog rock with rabbits round its hooves.
Why then, Daddy, did you shed
The pricey antlers of your Mayo accent
For the tree-felling voice of a harsh judiciary
Whose secret headquarters were in the Home Counties or High
   Germany?
Your son has gone back to Mayo to sleep with the island
   woman
Who talks so much she does not talk at all.
If he does not sleep with her, she will kill him – the pirate
   queen.

Poem Not Beginning with
a Line by Pindar

Having photocopied Goya by moonlight, the IRA
Hijacked a minibus on a circular road
In Armagh of the Nightingales,
Tromboned ten Protestant workmen into lining up
Along the footlights of the Armagh hills,
To kick high their legs, look left, look right,
And fed them such real midnight jazz
That not even Goya on a high
Could have improvised a tableau
Of such vaudeville terror, such prismatic carnage,
Bodies yearning over bodies,
Sandwich boxes, Thermos flasks, decks of playing cards.

Next morning at breakfast in the kitchen
I enquire of Daddy his judgment.
The President of the Circuit Court
Of the Republic of Ireland,
Appointed by the party of the Fine Gael,
Scooping porridge into his mouth,
Does not dissemble as he curls his lip,
Does not prevaricate as he gazes through me:
"Teach the Protestants a lesson,"
And, when I fail to reciprocate,
"The law is the law and the law must take its course."

"Teach the Protestants a lesson,"
That's what the man says,
The judge says,
The President of the Circuit Court

Of the Republic of Ireland says.
If you are mystified,
Dear Oxford University Reader in History,
What it reveals are not lacunae
But black holes
In your encyclopaedic knowledge
Of the roots of fascism in Ireland.
The party of the Fine Gael is the party
Of respectability, conformity, legitimacy, pedigree,
Faith, chivalry, property, virility,
The party of Collins, O'Higgins, O'Duffy, Cosgrave,
Great men queuing up at the bride's door.
Walk tall to the altar rail in pinstripe suit and silk tie.
Talk the language of men – bullshit, boob, cunt, bastard –
And – teach the Protestants a lesson.
The law is the law and the law must take its course.

Geronimo

Although we were estranged lovers
For almost thirty years,
When Daddy knew that he was going to die
He asked that we marry again.
After a reconciliation under a Scots
Pine in Palmerston Park
We remarried in the Church of St Aengus
In Burt, near Pluck.
In the navel of the Grianán of Aileach
We lay side by side on our backs
For the wedding photographs
Taken by a tall thin youth
With tresses of platinum grey hair
In a mauve suit and white sneakers.

We spent a second honeymoon
In the lakes of Sligo,
Putting up at the Ryan
Yeats Country Hotel
In Rosses Point,
A seaside hotel named after a poet
With special rates for families.
Throughout his life
Against all-comers
Daddy had maintained
That the lakes of Sligo
Were more scenic,
More bountiful, more placid,
More inscribed, more hallowed,

More inky, more papery,
More sensual, more ascetic,
More emblematic of what we are
Than the lakes of Killarney.

By the shores of Lough Arrow
In his eightieth year
At Ballindoon in the rain
In a two-light window
Of a roofless Dominican friary
He sat in profile
While I crouched behind a holly tree
Snapping him with my pocket Japanese camera.

By the shores of Lough Arrow
In his eightieth year
Among water-rolled stones with cranesbill
I spread out a tartan rug
For us to sit on and picnic
Listening to lakewater lapping,
Holding each other in one another's arms,
Resting our heads in one another's laps,
Hares springing up out of their own jackets.

For the umpteenth time
I told Daddy the story
Of Patrick Pearse's visit
To Daniel Corkery's house
In Cork City – the weather-slated
House by the Lough of Cork –
How Pearse solemnly informed Corkery
That the Lough's lakewater lapping
Had kept him from sleeping –
"A regrettable inconvenience," coughed Pearse.

Daddy loved to hear me
Tell that story and he'd hoo-hoo-hoo
Like a steam train chugging through Tír na nÓg.
He'd snort, "Tell me it again,"
And I'd tell him it again
And it was part of our liturgy
Of courtship and romance and marriage
That I should leave out bits
So that he could take a turn also
In the storytelling – we were a pair
Of choirboys among the rocks,
Chanting in orgy on a summer's morn
Our girlish devotion to the rain.
In the Corkery story, Daddy's line
Was the name of Corkery's novel
That celebrates the weather-slated house,
The Threshold of Quiet.

By the shores of Lough Arrow
In his eightieth year
At the cairn of Heapstown
While I stood atop the capstone
Daddy lay down in the uncut grass
And curled up like a foetus,
An eighty-year-old foetus.
"What are you doing?" I shouted down at him.
He made a face at me.
"Climbing goalposts," he shouted back up at me.

By the shores of Lough Arrow
In his eightieth year
Among the passage graves of Carrowkeel
In the Bricklieve Hills
He sat down in the bog cotton

And gazing north-west to Knocknarea
And to Deerpark and to Creevykeel
And to Ben Bulben and to Classiebawn
He began to weep in his laughter.
He wrapped his long white hair
Around his shoulders and refused
To utter for the rest of the day.
That night by the light
Of a golden-sepia half-moon
We walked the cliffs at Rosses Point,
Hand in hand among the actual shells.
He cupped my ear in his hands and whispered:
"Geronimo".
"I know," I said, "I know."

By the shores of Lough Arrow
In his eightieth year
In the main street of Ballinafad,
In the only street of Ballinafad,
On the steps of the Castle of the Curlews
He stood, and shaking out his brolly,
"You Curlew, you," he said.
"But for the red perch in the black stream
My life has been nothing, son.
Be good to your mother."

In the six months of white horses
Between our second honeymoon
And his deathdive
Geronimo's lovingkindness to me
Was as magnanimous as it was punctilious.
His last words to me were always,
"Be good to your mother – bring her
Flowers every day – what she likes

Above all is phlox."
As we shook hands and kissed
In the doorway, waiting for the elevator,
He'd add: "Don't be long."
I won't, Geronimo, I won't—be long.

"The Dream in the Peasant's Bent Shoulders"

You are sitting on a chair
Upright, moulded plastic,
At the end of your hospital bed
In the seventy-bed ward.
"Where are my pyjama bottoms?"
You cry at me, with a hoe in your hand,
A small, split cry.
When I fail to answer you, you cry,
"What have they done with my pyjama bottoms?"
"I don't know, Daddy, I don't know."

All I know
Is that you served the State
Unconditionally
For twenty-eight years
And that on this December afternoon in Dublin,
Without providing any reason or explanation,
They have taken away your pyjama bottoms.

Outside on Pearse Street
My mother weeps at the hospital gates.
Such was your loyalty to the State,
Your devotion and fidelity to the State,
You took Mother on one holiday only in twenty-eight years –
A pilgrimage by coach to the home of Mussolini
And Clara Petachi near Lago di Como,
A villa in the hills above Lago di Como.
Did you see in Mum your Clara?
Starlet, child bride, all négligé and tulle.

Loyalty to the State was the star
In the East of your life
And reward by the State.
Instead, they have taken away your pyjama bottoms
Leaving you only with your pyjama tops
And a hoe in your hand.
Your peasant's bent shoulders have ceased their dreaming
As you crouch down before me, a jewel in torment.
Out of willow eyes you stare at me.
"Hold my hand," you whisper.

A blond male doctor struts brusquely past
As we crouch here holding hands in twilight.
"Hold my hand," you whisper.
"I am holding your hand, Daddy," I respond.
But you do not hear me.
Clinging to your hoe
And gripping tightly my hand, you scream:
"*Hold my hand.*"

Glocca Morra

Dear Daughter – Watching my father die,
As one day you will watch me die,
In the public ward of a centre-city hospital,
Mid-afternoon bustle,
A transistor radio playing two or three beds away,
Paintwork flaking on the wall,
His breath dwindling,
His throat gurgling,
A source disappearing,
Source of all that I am before my eyes disappearing,
Well, watching your own father die slowly in front of you,
Die slowly right under your nose,
Is a bit like sitting in the front row of the concert hall
Watching a maestro performing Tchaikovsky's Grand Piano
    Sonata.
It's spectacular, so to speak,
But the audience feels helpless.

When Daddy died
I wrung my hands at the foot of his bed
Until a consultant doctor told me to stop it
And to show some respect for the dead.
The old prick.
He had done nothing for Daddy
Except pollute him with pills for twenty years
For fees in guineas.
They threw a sheet over him
And put screens around his bed
But I stood my ground

At the foot of the bed
While the transistor radio,
Like something hidden in a hedgerow,
Went on with its programme –
Rosemary Clooney crooning
"How are Things in Glocca Morra?"

Outside the ward window –
Which was in need of cleaning, I noticed –
The sun was going down in the west over the Phoenix Park
Where Daddy and me
("Daddy and I" – he corrects me –
He was a stickler for grammar),
Where Daddy and I
Played all sorts of games for years,
Football, hurling, cricket, golf, donkey,
Before he got into his Abraham-and-Isaac phase
And I got the boat to England
Before he had time to chop off my head
O Daddy dear –
As we find ourselves alone together for the last time,
Marooned in this centre-city hospital public ward,
I think that there is something consoling – cheerful, even –
About that transistor playing away in the next bed.
The day you bought your first transistor
You took us out for a drive in the car,
The Vauxhall Viva,
Down to a derelict hotel by the sea,
The Glocca Morra,
Roofless, windowless, silent,
And, you used add with a chuckle,
Scandalous.
You dandled it on your knee
And you stated how marvellous a gadget it was,

A portable transistor,
And that you did not have to pay
A licence fee for it,
You chuckled.
A man not much known for chuckling.
The Glocca Morra,
Roofless, windowless, silent and *scandalous*.

Rosemary Clooney —
The tears are lumbering down my cheeks, Dad —
She must be about the same age as you,
Even looks like you.
I bet her handwriting
Is much the same as yours,
You had a lovely hand,
Cursive, flourishing, exuberant, actual.
Whatever things are like in Glocca Morra
I'm sad that we're not going to be together any more.
Dear Daughter — When the time comes
For you to watch me die,
In a public place to watch me
Trickling away from you,
Consider the paintwork on the wall
And check out the music in the next bed.
"How are Things in Glocca Morra?"
Every bit as bad as you might think they are —
Or as good. Or not so bad. Love, Dad.

The Repentant Peter

AFTER FRANCISCO DE GOYA

Tonight is my forty-fifth birthday —
You are two years dead.
Last thing I do before getting into bed
Is kneel down beside bed
In my Marks & Spencer's women's pyjamas
Which I purchased thinking they were men's pyjamas,
A womanless man on a shopping spree.
Laying my head in my hands on the bed
I give thanks for the gift of life,
For your authorisation of me,
Your retrieval of my future,
An ape seeding himself in the Rift Valley.
I ask for forgiveness for my sins.

First time my wife saw me
Kneel down beside bed
She ate my head off
She was that shocked.
I do it
Because that is what you taught me to do.
I could not
Not do it.
You taught me that like you
I am destitute animal,
Frailer
Than plump lamb under candlelit chestnut,
Frailer
Than mother cat wheezing in cartwheel,
Frailer

Than galaxies of geese,
And that behind all my sanctimonious lechery,
It is all night, with only daylight above it.

Our Father

I was going over to Mummy's place for lunch.
I had said my morning prayers
But I had not expected
My morning prayers materially to alter the day.
Our Father who art in heaven
(Daddy had died two winters ago)
Hallowed be Thy name, Thy kingdom come,
Thy will be done on earth as it is in heaven.

I had decided to catch the number 13 bus to Palmerston Park
From outside Dáil Éireann in Kildare Street
But at the last moment I changed my mind
And I caught the number 14 bus to Dartry.
I do not know why I changed my mind.
Possibly it was because the number 14 came first
Or possibly it was because of the memory
That Daddy, when he was alive, appeared to be perplexed
That I never came home by the number 14 route.
He seemed to think that I should come home by the number 14
    route
And that it was a crime against nature
To come home by the number 13 route.

I sat at the back of the bus on the lower deck
With two bunches of flowers for Mummy in my lap.
When I became aware that the conductor was staring at me
We were stopped outside the National Concert Hall and I
    thought:
Maybe he likes the look of me.

He commented: "I like your irises."
"What?"
"Your irises—I like your irises."
The conductor swayed above me, a knowing smile in his eyes,
As the double decker lurched around Kelly's Corner—
A landmark of Daddy's
Because on it stood a pub called The Bleeding Horse.
It was the name that attracted him.
He was never inside it in his life.
Every time we drove past The Bleeding Horse
I stared at the blood trickling out of the white mare's withers,
All menstruation and still life.
"I love flowers"—the conductor continued,
Licking the baton of his forefinger—
"My wife says I'm mad and of course I am.
I am mad about flowers.
Lovely irises you have—let me touch them.
I have my own greenhouse—the width of this bus.
My father-in-law built it for me donkey's years ago.
My orchids are in bloom at the moment.
If I'd my way, I'd have nothing but orchids.
All the same a man's got to be pragmatic."
He clung lithely to the vertical rail as the driver
Flew the bus over Portobello Bridge.

"I've aubergines, peppers, tomatoes, lettuce.
The neighbours are keen on my iceberg lettuce.
They're always pestering me also for my courgettes.
Cucumber too—but you have to be cautious with cucumber.
What with the way the males pollinate the females
You've got to be terribly cautious with your stamens,
Cucumbers are very much that way inclined:
Proliferation, proclivities, you never know where you are.
I have to keep all my cacti on the upper shelves."

As we slowed down near Rathmines Town Hall, senior citizens
On Free Travel called out to the conductor to collect fares.
"Do your duty now, Mister, and collect fares."
But he waved to the passengers who were disembarking,
A wave that was at once a valediction and a benediction:
"I am not collecting fares this morning," he confided in me,
"There are times in public transport when it is more auspicious
Not to collect fares and today is an auspicious day.
I adore my greenhouse. It can get so hot inside it.
Anything more than a pair of shorts and I'm scalded.
'Where'd you get your tan?' – the neighbour woman asks me.
'In my greenhouse, where else?' – I answer her back.
A perfect lie.
She wags her finger at my magnolia in the front garden
And she teases me: 'Oh, a cherry blossom
Is good enough for the rest of us but not for the likes of you.
For the likes of you it has to be a *magnolium* no less.
Only a *magnolium* is good enough for the likes of you.'
That's what she calls it – a *magnolium*."

We were whizzing past the pharmacy on Upper Rathmines
    Road
And the Church of Ireland Teacher Training College
But he wanted to dwell on his magnolia:
"It's not a real word at all, you know, 'magnolia'.
There was a Frenchman – Magnol was his name –
From a place called Montpellier. My wife knew a man
From Montpellier – that's how I remember it.
But I do like your irises.
You have to be patient in this game
And it can be so tedious on top of that.
My grapes, for example. Grapes are too excitable.
I have to keep each grape separate from the other.
Time-consuming it is

Keeping all my grapes separate from each other.
Each grape has to be totally separate from the next grape
And only a few weeks ago I lost fifty pounds' worth
Of azaleas – wiped out by Jack Frost.
When I'm skedaddling off to the depot I ask the wife
To remember to open the greenhouse window
But if she remembers to open it,
Sure as not she will forget to close it.
You know what wives are like – not to mention husbands.
At the moment, actually, I'm all sweet pea."
I apologised to him as I dismounted at Dartry.
"Sorry, but I have to get out at this stop."
"Don't be sorry – be nice to your irises."

As the bus swerved away from the kerb, I thought:
Amn't I the lucky breadman that I got the Dartry bus
Instead of the Palmerston Park bus,
The number 14 instead of the number 13?
The conductor waved to me as the bus picked up speed.
I looked about me on the street to check if anybody was
    looking.
I blessed myself.
Our Father who art in heaven.
I could feel the conductor's knees brush against my lips
As he ran his fingers through the clay of my hair.

Under the chestnuts and the pine trees and the copper beeches
I walk down the street where Daddy slipped on the ice.
He had lain here until a gas worker had found him
And put him in an ambulance and waved goodbye to him,
A gas worker with a piece of piping in his hand.

I press the bell to Mummy's apartment.
I stare up into the surveillance camera lens.

I am a suspect in an interrogation centre,
A forty-five-year-old amoeba dwindling under a microscope.
When a light bulb flashes and her voice crackles over
The intercom I know she can perceive
The panic in the pupils of her son's eyes.
After lunch – soup, a chop, potatoes and peas –
She says that she does not understand my new book of poems
Which are poems I have composed for my dead father.
"But" – she smiles knowingly – "I like your irises."

Man Walking the Stairs

AFTER CHAIM SOUTINE

Odd to overhear that you think I am saying
"Man walking the stars"
When all my life I have been saying
"Man walking the stairs".

Living alone in a semi-detached villa
Between the mountains and the sea
I spend a great deal of time on the stairs.
Halfway up the stairs
I pause at the window overlooking
The entrance to our cul-de-sac,
The lancet window in our gable;
I pause or climb on.

When I get to the top of the stairs
I cannot remember why in the first place
I came up the stairs
But that is in the nature of living alone:
I am neither perplexed nor perturbed.
I go back downstairs and start
All over again, read another page,
Drink another cup of tea, hover
At the kitchen window, hover
At the front window, hover
In the hallway, hover
At the letterbox, hover
Before the looking-glass in the coat rack
That we bought in Christy Bird's for two-and-sixpence.

I know what it is I must do.
I must go back upstairs and search
Under my bed for that book I have mislaid –
The Oxford Dictionary of Quotations.
I am searching for a line from Donne:
"Make my dark poem light".
But I pause again at the gable window
This time to behold pine trees
Clutching at one another in a gale,
Pair of pines reprieved by the developer.

When I conquer the top of the stairs
I fall down the stairs,
All the way down to the foot of the stairs.
Lying at the foot of the stairs
For three days and three nights
I behold bills – gas bills
And telephone bills – Final Notices –
Swirl through the lips of the letterbox
And the attic trap door at the top of the stairs
Is flying, descending, circling, advancing.
It keeps getting closer to my face.
If they ever find me and I am still alive
They will accuse me of having been drinking,
Of having been at the sherry.
What is wrong with being at the sherry?
Pale dry sherry – her throat, her lips, her eyes.

I could never understand people
At any time but especially people
Advising me I ought to sell my home
Because of the stairs. "What you must do
Is to find yourself a convenient bungalow
And save yourself the stairs."

Like advising a man to swim in a pool with no water.
The whole point of my home
Is the stairs. Can you conceive
Of a life without stairs?

My life is the saga of a life on stairs.

When I was nine with my cousin William
Sliding down bannister rails
To crashland on beaches of linoleum
My father peering over cliffs down stairwells
Already unbuckling his trousers' belt.

From thirteen to seventeen years
I sat on the stairs keeping vigil
With myself and the stair rods
Watching through bannister uprights
My father and mother coming and going.
I could not speak to them
Because when I spoke I stammered.
I clung to the bannisters,
Creature of the stairs.

Marriage at twenty-three and seventeen years
Of hoovering the stairs;
A flight of stairs and a hoover
And I was the sainted spouse.
Upstairs mowing away, I could hear
My wife downstairs whistling away
Scanning the morning paper.

Stairs into stairs.

One stair at a time or
Three stairs at a time or
Four or five stairs at a time
In our forties when she and I
Were to our bedroom racing
In the middle of the day
Barely able to reach it in time,
Slipping, clambering, getting there,
Her arms around my knees,
Or to the bathroom to bathe
Together in the same bath and make
A mess of water on the floor;
A pot of phlox on the window sill
Or a cruet of lambs' tails from the hazel tree.

Days when we were not speaking
Or, truth to tell, days when
I was sulking and she kept out
Of my way, I'd sit all day
On the stairs, my knees tucked up
Under my chin, my elbows
Around my shinbones. I preferred
Sitting on stairs to sitting on chairs,
Sitting on the stairs facing the front door,
Facing south, facing south to the sea,
Remembering the Café Neptune in Batumi.

Man is the inventor of stairs.

How many miles of stairs
Have we walked together?
A great many, yet much less
Than the thousands of miles of stairs
I have walked alone.

I like to look around me on these long
Walks on the stairs;
Redwoods convulsed in gales, Scots pines,
Olive trees, sycamores, my wife's ashes.

Man walking the stairs.
Man doing nothing else
Except walking the stairs.
Man scattering his wife's ashes
Either side of the stairs.
Sower stalking the stairs.

Our only son lived a long
And good life, only to be
Knocked down by a motorcar
On Leeson Street Bridge.
We buried him in the front garden
Along with our two black cats.
I think of him on the stairs –
How he used crawl face forwards
Down the stairs if I promised
To catch him at the foot of the stairs.

I carry my stairs in my arms
Up through the treetops of Provence,
All my treads and all my raisers.
Love is not love that is not courtly;
That's what every woman knows.

Man walking the stairs
Is man treading water.
Our house of water:
Do not open the door.

Odd to overhear that you think I am saying
"Man walking the stars"
When all my life I have been saying
"Man walking the stairs".

The Virgin and Child

AFTER LORENZO GHIBERTI

My mother is as much
A virgin at seventy-five
As she was at seventeen;
As much a small
Stream going nowhere;
As much a small
Ocean going everywhere;
Terracotta moon
In pink nightie.

When I visit her
In her apartment
In the solitary suburbs,
I jump up into her arms.
She hugs me, holding me up
With her left hand under my bottom:
"O my curly headed
Little golden wonder
What has become of you?"

Once a virgin mother
Always a virgin mother.
In my forty-seventh year
My virgin mother cradles me in her arms;
A brief trout of a frown
Jumps up
The brief weir of her face.

Mother most lost;
Mother most found.
Mother most dogged;
Mother most frail.
Mother most peripheral;
Mother most central.

Truth is, son,
You and I as a pair
Are, were, always will be
Out on a limb,
Outcasts in terracotta;
Refugees in clay.

The Riding School

AFTER KAREL DUJARDIN

Dung, cobble, wall, cypress;
Delight in art whose end is peace;
No cold-eyed horseman of the Irish skies
Can compare with me
Leading out the Grey of the Blues.

I in my red blanket
Under the Cave Hill Mountain
Leading out the Grey of the Blues:
The blindness of history in my eyes;
The blindness of history in my hands.

To get up at four every morning
And to lead out the Grey of the Blues;
Delight in art whose end is peace;
Hold his reins with my eyes open;
His dappled hindquarters;
His summer coat;
His knotted mane;
His combed-out tail;
His swanface;
His bullneck;
His spineline;
His tiny, prancing grace-notes.

And I in my red blanket
Under the Cave Hill Mountain
Leading out the Grey of the Blues:
The blindness of history in my eyes;
The blindness of history in my hands.

223

I take pride in my work;
Delight in art whose end is peace;
The way I lead out a song;
The way I hold the reins of a song in my hands
Between my stubby fingers.
I talk to my song;
My song talks to me.
In the blackest weathers
We have our sunniest hours.
How many early mornings
In black rain I have talked my song
Round and round the pink paddock!

I in my red blanket
Under the Cave Hill Mountain
Leading out the Grey of the Blues:
The blindness of history in my eyes;
The blindness of history in my hands.

My song is nearing the end of its tether;
Lament in art whose end is war;
Opera glasses, helicopters, TV crews;
Our slayings are what's news.
We are taking our curtain call,
Our last encore.
True to our natures
We do not look into the camera lenses
But at one another.
In a gap of oblivion, gone.

I in my red blanket
Under the Cave Hill Mountain
Leading out the Grey of the Blues:
The blindness of history in my eyes;
The blindness of history in my hands.

The Knucklebone Player

AFTER GUSTAV NATORP

Two years after Paul died
I met Nuala cycling in the park
With Saturday's *Irish Times*
In her front-wheel basket.
We fell to chatting about Paul:
What a cheerful, solitary fellow he was.
I asked her if there was anything of his
She would like as a souvenir,
Keepsake, relic.
After all – in the middle of all –
He had been her partner.
She whistled, nostalgically.

She said: I would like his knucklebones.
Both knucklebones?
Both knucklebones.
I promised her that the next time
The grave was opened
I would keep an eye out for Paul's knucklebones.

His father's death gave me the opportunity
To sift the soil for Paul's knucklebones.
One evening's sifting in late spring
Threw up both knucklebones.
I sealed them in a Jiffy bag,
A cassette-sized Jiffy bag;
Dropped it through Nuala's letterbox.

Down the Hole-in-the-Wall,
Midsummer's day,
Strolling past the sunworshippers,
I came upon Nuala topless
And poised, sitting up in the sand
Playing with something in her right hand,
Her left foot in her left hand,
Her hair tied up in a bun.

In a slow, low voice –
Reminiscent of the phonograph recording
Of Oscar Wilde's rendition
Of "The Ballad of Reading Gaol" –
She called me over:
"Each woman kills
The man she loves."

Obscurely I could see
That what she was rattling
In the palm of her hand
Were Paul's knucklebones.
She was playing dice
With Paul's knucklebones.

Demurely, she giggled: I have a friend –
A wood carver, a previous lover.
I commissioned him to make dice
Out of Paul's knucklebones:
"A throw of the dice
Never abolishes chance."

I accepted her invitation
To share her lunch,
To play dice with her.

Sitting opposite her on her towel,
A lettuce leaf between my teeth,
I stared – she swallowed my stare whole –
Into her eyes prancing up and down
The low fences of her breasts,
Her dilated never-pass-a-man eyes.

I said: Nuala –
You are a born knucklebone player.
She whistled: I am –
I am a born knucklebone player.

Flower Girl, Dublin

AFTER JACK B. YEATS

Afternoons in winter
I sit in Robert Roberts Café
Watching men and women,
Especially women.
I am crazy about women.

Just because I am a man without a woman
Does not mean that I have no interest in women.
In fact, I am preoccupied with fundamentally nothing else.
I read all of Nietzsche when I was seventeen.
Then it was time to grow up.

Would you please hose some of your hot liquid into me?
Mother of five to boy at coffee dispenser.
She must be forty at least but as she sips her grounds –
Her Costa Rican grounds –
As she smacks her lips
Trickling her tongue tip along her lip rim
She is a girl not yet nineteen
Haughty as an Englishwoman in Shanghai.
Red cloche hat, grey wool overcoat,
Black low high-heel shoes.

I see in today's newspaper a black-and-white photograph
Of a woman in a black miniskirt at the opening
Of the Seán McSweeney Retrospective last night
(There is a man who can paint – not many can
Since the Great Yeat died in 1957).

But much as that photo causes a stir in me –
An abstract stir in me –
It is as nothing compared to this glimpse of ankle –
Ankle –
Of the mother of five in red cloche hat –
Would you please hose some of your hot liquid into me?

Time to go – home. I dally to loiter
In the doorway of the café eyeing myself
In the shop window opposite, my bowler hat,
My frock coat, my gleaming galoshes.
A flower girl with a single red rose in her hands
Is passing the time of day with the mother of five
Not making any particular pitch to sell.

Timorousness entices me to my right –
But I know, Jack, I know
I should step briskly to my left,
Proffer the single red rose to the mother of five,
Nail my colours to the mast.
Will I or won't I?
And give all my loose change to the flower girl –
All my loose change?

Grief

AFTER JACK B. YEATS

I

I am a man;
All that is human is alien to me.

I insert my penis gun into your mouth and –
As the quaint old mantra has it –
"Blow your brains out".

How I delight to behold
At evening by the campfire on the seashore
After our games of softball
The wild, wild hedgerows'
Fuchsia of your dripping brains:

Oilily –
When I drop my Judaeo-Christian trousers,
Spread out my legs across the Islamic sky,
Drop my droppings on you.

What I admire most about myself,
What I most cherish
In my children's bedrooms
As I lull their cradles,
Is my own ordure.

A man's own ordure
Is the basis of culture;
In the hi-tech of my ordure
Ticks the future of my futurelessness.

My golden locks
Are things of the past.

I am a man;
All that is human is alien to me.

II

I was on the Dublin–Cork train minding my own business
When a not-so-young man opposite me – about the same age as
    myself –
Put down his paper and asked me without a by-your-leave
"What class of occupation are you in yourself?"
To my surprise I answered him:
"I am an art gallery attendant."

I can still hear myself saying it:
"I am an art gallery attendant" –
Has a ring to it.
The beautiful thing was that it shut him up.
We were only pulling out of Kildare
But he did not open his mouth again
The whole way down to Cork.

I am an art gallery attendant
In the National Gallery of Ireland.
I am the man
Who sits under "Grief"
At the head of the Gallery
Watching fleets of feet paddling towards me.
If anyone asks me what "Grief" means
I say I do not know what "Grief" means.
That is the truth. I do not know what "Grief" means.
I do not think anyone knows what "Grief" means.
It is a pretty picture – that is all I know about "Grief"

After having sat under it for twenty-five years
And I think that is all anybody knows about "Grief".

Another thing that I do not understand
Is people who make a racket with their footwear on the parquet.
It never fails to grate on my nerves.
What's in it for a body to wantonly introduce
Noise into a place of worship?
It's like people who say you can accommodate wars
When obviously there is no way you can accommodate wars
Or people who see fit to bite hard-boiled sweets in cinemas.
I suppose it's something inherent in society and the individual,
Crowds and power.
That is what I often think
Sitting here under "Grief".

People often ask me also the way to the Restaurant.
By the time they have finished asking me
They have spotted it and they apologise
For having asked me in the first place.
By this time they have caught a glimpse of "Grief".
They stop in their tracks. They stare up at it
Like as if they have seen a horse come through the wall.
All of us hanging about in the parade ring at a race meeting.
Nervously, they approach it and at the last moment they make
A dive into the corner to sniff the label.
They canter up and down the length of the picture
Before standing back out again in the middle –
Connections in the middle of the parade ring –
Pleased with themselves to be at the centre of the picture,
Yet anxious to get back outside again and to watch –
Or not to watch, as the case may be – from a safe distance.
"Grief". I scratch my chin. They scamper off for their coleslaw.
Punters scoff a lot of coleslaw in the National Gallery of Ireland.

Woman of the Mountain

On the occasion of the inauguration of
President Mary Robinson, 3 December, 1990

Politics . . . the art of the impossible, that is the art of
making both ourselves and the world better.

VÁCLAV HAVEL, New Year's Day 1990

I

Do bhí bean uasal . . .
Girl in winter at her bedroom window in the rooftops,
All seven years of her,
Gazing down across the River Moy at St Muredach's Cathedral,
Moorish arch under snow,
Old Man curled up in cathedral porch.

II

Old Man gets back up onto his feet, yawns, shivers,
Beats his wings,
Opens his overcoat, a grandfather clock
Adjusting his pendulum, tugs at his waistcoat,
Smoothes down his beard, dons his railwayman's cap,
Buttons up, slings a sack over his shoulder,
Picks up his walking stick, stands vertical,
Hands by his sides, lips sealed, opens wide his eyes,
Begins to lift up off the snow at an angle
Of forty-five degrees. He ascends, tick-tock,
Past her bedroom window.

III

Downstairs, her brother Aubrey is on the telephone from
  Paris
Telling his mother that he's not really lonely in the Collège des
  Irlandais,
That it's snowing in Paris also and that he's not really homesick,
That Paris is as beautiful as Ballina and he trusts all the family
  are well.
His mother tells him that she's made curtains for his room.
She'll parcel them by express post tomorrow.
Curtains'll help to keep in the heat, make his room home-like.

IV

Next day up town with her mother she spots
Old Man in the porch of the Post Office.
Mother, that man flew past my bedroom window yesterday
Making a tick-tocking noise.

Licking the blue *Par Avion* sticker, her mother confides:
That man's the man who lives on a wing and a prayer.
His name's John but they call him Nephin
Because he spends so much time talking to the mountain,
Listening to the mountain.
His conversation is sweetness itself.
In his young days he was a lawyer – quite a brilliant lawyer –
But he gave up the law for the mountain.
First thing he does every morning is to step outside
To check how the mountain is.
Good morning, branch-of-my-tree!
How the mountain looks to him, what the mountain says to
  him,
Ordains the texture of his day.

Nothing bedevils him – poverty, age,
Disease, death, bad luck – none of it
Bedevils him, always in the best of form.
He winds himself up every night with a prayer.
Nobody enjoys life more in Ballina than Nephin.
No wonder you saw him fly past your bedroom window
Making a tick-tocking noise.

Digging out of her mother a Kleenex tissue and a blue Bic
    biro,
She asks Old Man for his autograph.
He smiles at her through fritters of freckles:
Mary, the day you become Uachtarán na hÉireann
Come see me in my sweet shop under the mountain.
I'll embrace you with all my wings, all my prayers.

V

Having express posted the curtains, her mother takes her
    hand
And, as they saunter back down the town past the Bolero and
    Moylett's Corner,
Hums: Curtains'll keep him warm, make the room home-like.

Old Man, with his wings in his overcoat pockets, snorts:
"How's himself in Paris?" – adding the answer –
"Salmon fishing from on top of the Eiffel Tower."

VI

On the corner of the Rue des Irlandais
Her brother gazes up at the street name plaque,
Discerning behind it its original name –
Rue du Cheval Vert.

She swears to herself in her sleep,
A figure of candlelight in water:
I will live all the days of my life
For my brother in Paris on his green horse;
I will live all the days of my life
For Old Man homeless in Mayo, Africa;
I will live all the days of my life
Looking out of my window;
Never will I not look out of my porthole
No matter how well fed the lamb on the table,
No matter how urgent the jet.
I will live all the days of my life
Keeping faith with the mountain:
The mountain as snail;
The mountain as tree.
The mountain as city;
The mountain as sleep.
The mountain as programme;
The mountain as programmer.
Mother Mountain;
Father Mountain.
I will keep vigil all the nights of my life
Under a clock with wings.
Good morning, branch-of-my-tree!

The Dublin–Paris–Berlin–Moscow Line

I am a Dubliner
For whom Ithaca
Is Dublin Bay at twilight as I tighten my seatbelt,
A Fokker 50 dropping down the Kish
To roar in low past Howth.
From the Sugar Loaf to the Poolbeg to Ballymun Towers,
My native tongue:
Licking the roof of my mouth, the rim of your lip.
At midnight, I kiss the ground of your throat.

I want to live with you
In the light of things as they are;
In the light of the Festival of the City of Culture
The saga of which I will tell to my daughters;
In the light of the homeless children of Asia;
In the light of the beggar women of Nassau Street;
In the light of my loneliness;
In the light of my anonymity;
In the light of my non–identity;
To dwell in a world without rhetoric;
In the silence of my own song;
In the voice of my own memory;
In a milieu of agèd couples
Teetering on the brink of the Jardin du Luxembourg;
In a choir of atheists in Saint-Sulpice;
Attila the Dove cooing in the treetops of Saint-Sulpice
"Never praise the victors":
In Europe at the Gates of Asia.

I worship Christ with a flute, not with a knife.

When the Festival is over –
Farewell to Claudio and Mavis and Bert, Daniela and Oleg –
I turn the key on Dublin
And, dropping the key in the Seine,
Dream of the key also sinking down into its bed.
I take the train from Saint-Lazare to Caen
And a bus from Caen to Lion-Sur-Mer
Where in the Hôtel de la Plage I fall
Into the arms of my daughters.
In the circumstances, they are understanding
And they pick me up
And they take me for long walks on the Normandy beaches
Listening good-humouredly to my Festival saga:
Potholes, Dad, potholes.

May I, a Dubliner, live always in exile
In the village of Ringsend between the Drain and the Gut;
May I lack always a consistent vision of the universe
When I am saying my poems;
May I remain always inarticulate
When I am composing my poems;
May I belong always to the oral tradition
Who is a woman keeping her man on his toes:
She permits him to speak solely from memory.

May I never again fall
Out of the arms of my daughters
As we tramp up and down Europe
Having become the migrants that we are –
Barbarians on the Dublin–Paris–Berlin–Moscow line.
From the shores of the Aran Islands
To the foothills the far side of the Caucasus

These are the terraced streets
That smell of home to us.
May I be an actual nobody –
In Mayo serving burgers.

In a cinema in Tbilisi,
We sit licking ice creams
Watching a black-and-white documentary
Of *The Woman's Daughter* by Dermot Bolger.
On the plane back to Moscow,
Flying over the Caucasus,
I repine in the porthole of an Aeroflot jet
And I confide to the man's father, Anthony Cronin,
The first Dubliner I met in my life,
Staring down at the Caucasian peaks below us:
"They are *like* tents."
With restraint he grimaces:
"Paul, will you please stop
Saying that things are *like* things.
Either things are – or they are not."

Faith Healer

to Donal McCann

I

First night of *Faith Healer* at the Abbey Theatre
I walk on water into the bar;
Acquaintances of acquaintances of acquaintances
Pushing me from one to t'other;
Knocking me down on the floor;
Picking me up off the floor
Only again to knock me down on the floor.

My spectacles get knocked off my nose.
When I bend to pick them up off the floor
An accountant shoves me from behind;
An auctioneer shoves me from the front;
A solicitor shoves me from the side;
A gallery owner puts his two arms around me.
When I demur, they cajole me:
Why do you react like an infant child?
Why take yourself so seriously?

II

Not like, but am, an infant child.
What I take so seriously's the play.
Who knows who my mother is?
Who knows who my father is?
Every fallen birch leaf of it.

I want to kneel down under the play;
Under the jagged stars of its stillness;

240

Under its torrents of chatter
As they freeze before my eyes;
I want to kneel down in my seat
And be prayed over, and pray;
I want to keel over;
I want to lie down with the frost
Before its final surrender,
Before its final sunrise;
I want to be sleet in daylight.

I want to pray at the footlights
Where in the dark night of my grave
I have seen the candle flame
Become an exculpated face
Explaining my fate to me:
A flame in all its facets of flight;
An infant child in a hole in the ground;
A nimbus of ashes in a post hole;
A circle of cows peering down at me.

I want to hear the play confide in me
After the play has ended.
I want to meet my mother and father
On their way home from my grave,
Going home to Kinlochbervie.
I want to rest with the rest
On the Rest on the Flight into Egypt.
I want to eat Rembrandt Bread,
Friel Potato Cake.

III

First night of my grave
I want to stand alone centre stage,

241

Gaze out into the wings either side of me,
Flies of blood
Which are my wings also,
Webbed wings of my hands,
These hands which are all that I am and you are,
Fingertip to fingertip,
Thumb to opposable thumb.

To be seen for whom I am and you are:
Infant child;
My snail's slime glistening from era to era;
An actor alone in his dressing room;
A playwright in a jam jar;
Acquaintances of acquaintances of acquaintances;
Deposed, somnolent, cruciform.

In the bar of the Abbey, I lie down on the floor
At my own pace;
First-night faces peering down at me,
All fezes and tassels;
What will you have? What would you like?
Give me some water and let me die a little.

In my watery grave
I mind and do not mind
What you say about me —
I who was born in Kinlochbervie.
To be wholly alive is to be wholly dead.

27 November 1990

A Spin in the Rain with Seamus Heaney

You had to drive across to Donegal town
To drop off a friend at the Dublin bus
So I said I'd come along for the spin –

A spin in the rain.
Bales of rain
But you did not alter your method of driving,

Which is to sit right down under the steering wheel
And to maintain an upwards-peering posture
Treating the road as part of the sky,

A method which motoring correspondents call
Horizontal-to-the-vertical.
The hills of Donegal put down their heads

As you circled upwards past their solitary farmhouses,
All those agèd couples drenched over firesides,
Who once were courting couples in parked cars.

You parked the car in Donegal town and we walked the
    shops –
Magee's Emporium and The Four Masters Bookshop.
You bought ice-cream cones. I bought women's magazines.

We drove on up through the hills past Mountcharles
And Bruckless and Ardara.
There was a traffic jam in Ardara,

Out of which you extricated yourself
With a jack-knife U-turn on a hairpin bend
With all the bashful panache of a cattle farmer —

A cattle farmer who is not an egotist
But who is a snail of magnanimity,
A verbal source of calm.

Back in the Glenties you parked outside the National School
Through whose silent classrooms we strayed,
Silent with population maps of the world.

Standing with our backs to a deserted table-tennis table
We picked up a pair of table-tennis bats
And, without being particularly conscious of what we were at,

We began to bat the ball one to the other
Until a knock-up was in progress,
Holding our bats in pen grips.

So here we are playing a game of ping-pong
Which is a backdrop to our conversation
While our conversation is a backdrop to our game.

We are talking about our children and you speak
Of the consolation of children when they grow up
To become our most trusted of all companions.

I could listen to you speak along these lines
For the rest of the day and I dare say
You could listen to me also speak along my lines:

I have always thought that ping-pong balls –
Static spheres fleet as thoughts –
Have flight textures similar to souls'.

I note that we are both of us
No mean strikers of the ball and that, although
We have distinct techniques of addressing the table –

Myself standing back and leaping about,
Yourself standing close and scarcely moving –
What chiefly preoccupies us both is spin.

As darkness drops, the rain clears.
I take my leave of you to prepare my soul
For tonight's public recital. Wishing each other well.

Poetry! To be able to look a bullet in the eye,
With a whiff of the bat to return it spinning to drop
Down scarcely over the lapped net; to stand still; to stop.

The Toll Bridge

to Francis Stuart on his ninetieth birthday

I

The woman in the toll
Down at the Toll Bridge —
Furry creature, big ears, snub nose —
A moose she is —
A moose under a bus —
Is teasing me
For having my meter on with my taxi empty.
I am delivering a book — I advise her —
Northside to southside.

When she enquires the name of the book and I enlighten her,
She states that I will have to pay her a toll on it.
I know she is teasing me but I pay her a toll on it.
I like paying her the toll — paying her any toll —
Having to fling the toll into her empty basket
Or having to lean out of the driver's seat window
And deposit my coin into the palm of her hand.
She reiterates the book's name: "*A Hole in the Head*."
I reiterate the author's name: "Francis Stuart."

II

It became our passion.
I scoured the bookshops of Dublin City for a copy.
None of them had it. They said that it was "Out of Print",
That there was "a question mark over Francis Stuart".
She peered down at me from her perch in the toll:
A question mark over Francis Stuart?

Why don't you nick me a copy?
Nick you a copy?
From the party you delivered it to.
If there is a question mark over Francis Stuart
I would like to partake of Francis Stuart;
A man with a question mark over him
Might be a man with ninety question marks over him.

III

The party had an address in Dundrum.
I remembered him because he answered the door
In a seaman's polo-neck navy-blue knitted pullover
Holding in his hands a white rabbit.
I decided to call on him, ask him for a loan of
A Hole in the Head.
I felt ill waiting for him to answer the door;
As it happened, on that particular night, dejected.
But talking to him was like talking to one of the old masters
If you can envisage the old masters as being Japanese
— The red horse at the black well —
— The boy on the mountain —
— The sea in flower —
And I came away from him with bunches of new skates in both
    hands.

When I reported to him our passion he asked me her name.
When I told him I did not know her name
He said that that was how it should always be —
That it was better for a man and a woman
Not to know one another's names;
That it was better for a man and a woman
Never to know one another's names,
The thing in passion being anonymity.

He held out the rabbit to me.
I was afraid, but I took it.
He held my head in his hands—
His hands warm from rabbit fur.
He ran his fingers through my hair
Before sinking a forefinger
Down into the slime of my brain.
He whispered: The hole in your head.
When he bowed his dark head of white hair
I could decipher the profile of the nimbus
Round the hole in his own head:
A full moon on a cloudy night.

He loaned me the book—
On condition that I never gave it back to him.

IV

She, in her turn, when I gave it to her
Made it a condition of our passion
That we would never address one another
By one another's names
And that I would continue to pay her the toll,
Continue always to pay her the toll.

Although our passion continues to grow
And we can do things that we used not be able to do
And what we do now we do better,
I never miss a chance to drive back down along
The Toll Bridge
At night—late at night—
And pay her my toll.
The Toll Bridge
Is our dovecote, our ghetto, our haunt, our suburb, our ark—
Our ark of the north on the south bank of the Liffey.

We chat and she drops my coin on her floor
And she is saying: What does it mean to be a writer?
I jump out of my taxi and climb up into the toll with her
And we get down on the floor on our hands and knees
And search for my coin.
I say to her: To be a writer is to be nothing.
Nothing in my life has vouchsafed me such gold dust
As to get down on my hands and knees on the floor with her
Searching for my coin.

Swapping straws we suck.
She shivers: I will stay in Ringsend.
We leave it at that
But on feast nights —
Storytellings, homecomings, pay packets, new licence plates —
She shudders: I will go back to Berlin.
She swears: Christ, I set eyes on him once.
At the beginning of the film *Wings of Desire* —
Der Himmel über Berlin —
He was standing on top of the broken tower
Of the Gedächtniskirche
In a navy-blue overcoat with wings,
Aged about forty, and a voice said:
"If mankind loses its storyteller
It will lose its childhood."

V

I squint down into the hole in her head.
I stick my tongue into the hole in her head.
I shout out into the hole in her head:
Stop all traffic;
Drop down all the poles of the Toll Bridge.
I lope out into the centre of the plaza at the Toll Bridge —

A snail in my prime –
And, my soul all humility and periphery,
I proclaim to the Republic of Ireland and Ulster,
My cosmos, my ice rink:
Finally, I bequeath to you this painting
Which henceforth will be the only priceless
Painting in our national collection in Merrion Square West.
It is by Francis Bacon
When he was a vagabond in Provence with Vincent Van Gogh
Seeking asylum from mankind
And it has been hanging in a woman poet's bedroom in Berlin
Since the year 1944.
It is Bacon's masterpiece and it is entitled
"A Question Mark over Francis Stuart".
As you will observe,
It is Bacon's intaglio of the postmodernist halo.

Shall these bones live?
With a sickle in one hand and a satsuma in the other hand
Francis Stuart is dicing himself into portions
Feeding the birds at the Toll Bridge,
Sparrows on the fenders of Fiestas;
Feeding the leopards at the Toll Bridge,
Strays in the rear mirrors of Fiats;
The poles lift up;
And the horns do not too harshly blow –
Do not too harshly wind up their themes:
Driver, driver; improvise, improvise.

A Hole in the Head is all that I implore;
A Hole in the Head with Charity in Paris.
A Hole in the Head is all that I implore;
A Hole in the Head with Charity in Paris.

29 April 1992

The Only Man Never to Meet
Samuel Beckett

That young American-Irish woman on the brink of everything
In a secondhand Alsatian waiter's black jacket,
Ankle-length pink bolero skirt
At the flea market at the Porte de Montreuil,
Coffees afterwards on the sidewalk in the sun
"Hope is a knave befools us evermore . . ."
Had we met
We might never have known one another as we did:
Her death — and his, and mine.

How lucky I was never to meet Samuel Beckett.

1981 — the year I spent working in the Collège des Irlandais
5 rue des Irlandais
Paris 5
Persons were always plotting
For me to meet Samuel Beckett.

In my cell on the third floor
I used wake up in sweats
With Samuel Beckett at my bedside
Peering at me.
I'd plead with him to soak my facecloth
(There was a tiny washhandbasin in the corner of my cell)
And I'd poultice my visage with it
Whispering to him: Go away.
But he'd whisper back:
Won't go away.

Despite all plotting

I succeeded in not meeting Samuel Beckett.

While I have myself to thank

I think that Samuel Beckett also ought to be thanked;

That Samuel Beckett was as lucky not to have met me

As I was lucky not to have met him:

Her death – and his, and mine.

The Soldier

On the road back to Dublin from Galway
I picked up a man outside Ballinasloe.
Before we had got to Athlone – sixteen miles on –
He had admitted to me that he was separated from his wife
And I had admitted to him that I was separated from my
    husband.
Passing through Tyrellspass he confided in me that he was an
    alcoholic.
To which I replied that I also am an alcoholic.
He had a pair of rosary beads
Twined round the fingers of his right hand
And he fed them all the way back to Dublin –
Feeding the beads through his long, narrow fingers,
Paying them in, paying them out.
In a Sunday night traffic jam
On the outskirts of Maynooth
I asked him:
What are your beads made of?
He howled: Moonstones.
He explained that when there is a full moon,
If you are wearing moonstones,
You can see into the future.
He asked me to drop him off in Lucan
And, as I dropped him, I drove up onto the kerb
I was that – that mystified.
That night, thinking about him in bed,
I realized that he was a soldier
Come back from, or going to, the wars.
A gentleman with no hope – no hope at all.

My Belovèd Compares Herself
to a Pint of Stout

When in the heat of the first night of summer
I observe with a whistle of envy
That Jackson has driven out the road for a pint of stout,
She puts her arm around my waist and scolds me:
Am I not your pint of stout? Drink me.
There is nothing except, of course, self-pity
To stop you also having your pint of stout.

Putting self-pity on a leash in the back of the car,
I drive out the road, do a U-turn,
Drive in the hall door, up the spiral staircase,
Into her bedroom. I park at the foot of her bed,
Nonchalantly step out leaving the car unlocked,
Stroll over to the chest of drawers, lean on it,
Circumspectly inspect the backs of my hands,
Modestly request from her a pint of stout.
She turns her back, undresses, pours herself into bed,
Adjusts the pillows, slaps her hand on the coverlet:
Here I am — at the very least
Look at my new cotton nightdress before you shred it
And do not complain that I have not got a head on me.

I look around to see her foaming out of the bedclothes
Not laughing but gazing at me out of four-leggèd eyes.
She says: Close your eyes, put your hands around me.
I am the blackest, coldest pint you will ever drink
So sip me slowly, let me linger on your lips,
Ooze through your teeth, dawdle down your throat,
Before swooping down into your guts.

While you drink me I will deposit my scum
On your rim and when you get to the bottom of me,
No matter how hard you try to drink my dregs—
And being a man, you will, no harm in that—
I will keep bubbling up back at you.
For there is no escaping my aftermath.
Tonight—being the first night of summer—
You may drink as many pints of me as you like.
There are barrels of me in the tap room.
In thin daylight at nightfall,
You will fall asleep drunk on love.
When you wake early in the early morning
You will have a hangover,
All chaste, astringent, aflame with affirmation,
Straining at the bit to get to first mass
And holy communion and work—the good life.

Woman Footballer of the Year

AFTER SARAH DURCAN

On a summer's night in 1991
In a football tournament in Ringsend Park
She scored a goal with her knee –
How off balance she was when she scored that goal with her
    knee!

After we are all dead and gone,
The ball soaring into the net,
Her knee under the pathologist's scalpel
Watched over by faces of millions of parents, friends, relations,
    strangers.

She was more or less always off balance
When she scored goals – that was her temperament
As well as her technique.
Her mother before her with stones in her pockets scored goals
    with both knees.

On the limelit sidelines, we fathers with bicycles,
Brandishing our arms, rolling our heads;
My head no longer my head, my arm no longer my arm;
The sun getting ready to go down behind the city into the quiet
    quiet morgues.

The game was almost over.
In the heat of the summer's night
She had shed all her gear
Except for one long laddered black stocking on her left leg.

It was with that same raw tibia
In Mercurochrome – parcelled up, tagged,
As we spectators saw it –
That in slow motion she kneed the ball into the net.

In that instant she was an airborne donkey,
A birch tree being felled,
A kicked-up snail,
An oystershell tossed from a railway carriage any old where
    between Badenweiler and Moscow.

If a married woman can ever be said to be married,
In that instant she was a married woman;
All alone out there in the universe doing the business;
Making an ass of herself.

Gaping at the priest at the consecration,
Lifting up the host high above his head,
What I am seeing is a woman footballer
Kneeing space into an empty net to the barking of Ballsbridgers
    and the cheers of Ringsenders.

I am the woman footballer of the year,
Only the righteous can squash me;
I am the woman footballer of the year,
Only the righteous can squash me.

My Daughter Síabhra in Moscow, 19 August 1991

Monday lunchtime
At the Edinburgh Book Festival
Meandering the marquees
In Charlotte Square.
Dermot Bolger,
In his hand *The Journey Home*,
Yells down a duckboard-walk:
Gorbachev's gone!

Phone calls to the Irish
Department of Foreign Affairs.
No lines to Moscow.
All afternoon at the tiny
TV in my hotel room
Watching the tanks in Moscow.

Father fretting for his daughter,
Yet pleased she is at the heart of things
Learning Russian. Next morning,
Telegram from Moskva:
THERES BEEN SOME SORT OF COUP DETAT TANKS ON THE
     STREET IM FINE DONT WORRY LOVE SIABHRA

II

We are caught up in a family civil war
When you fly back into Dublin on August 30th.
By virtue of your Bulgakovian midwifery

We manage to induce a truce
Although not until eight months later
When at your prodding
We all get together to attend *The Cherry Orchard*
In a theatre over a maternity hospital.

Thanks to you I get to know
Chekhov's untranslatable word for a human being –
You Nothing you –
And to see Cyril Cusack at eighty-two
Playing the eighty-seven-year-old Nothing.
Dear Daughter – After all that has transpired,
All that I aspire to be is Nothing.
So, at my deathbed, you will smile:
You Nothing you!

Father's Day, 21 June 1992

Just as I was dashing to catch the Dublin-Cork train,
Dashing up and down the stairs, searching my pockets,
She told me that her sister in Cork wanted a loan of the axe;
It was late June and
The buddleia tree in the backyard
Had grown out of control.
The taxi was ticking over outside in the street,
All the neighbours noticing it.
"You mean that you want me to bring her down the axe?"
"Yes, if you wouldn't mind, that is –"
"A simple saw would do the job, surely to God
She could borrow a simple saw."
"She said that she'd like the axe."
"OK. There is a Blue Cabs taxi ticking over outside
And the whole world inspecting it,
I'll bring her down the axe."
The axe – all four-and-a-half feet of it –
Was leaning up against the wall behind the settee –
The fold-up settee that doubles as a bed.
She handed the axe to me just as it was,
As neat as a newborn babe,
All in the bare buff.
You'd think she'd have swaddled it up
In something – if not a blanket, an old newspaper,
But no, not even a token hanky
Tied in a bow round its head.
I decided not to argue the toss. I kissed her goodbye.

The whole long way down to Cork
I felt uneasy. Guilt feelings.
It's a killer, this guilt.
I always feel bad leaving her
But this time it was the worst.
I could see that she was glad
To see me go away for a while,
Glad at the prospect of being
Two weeks on her own,
Two weeks of having the bed to herself,
Two weeks of not having to be pestered
By my coarse advances,
Two weeks of not having to look up from her plate
And behold me eating spaghetti with a knife and fork.
Our daughters are all grown up and gone away.
Once when she was sitting pregnant on the settee
It snapped shut with herself inside it,
But not a bother on her. I nearly died.

As the train slowed down approaching Portarlington
I overheard myself say to the passenger sitting opposite me:
"I am feeling guilty because she does not love me
As much as she used to, can you explain that?"
The passenger's eyes were on the axe on the seat beside me
"Her sister wants a loan of the axe . . ."
As the train threaded itself into Portarlington
I nodded to the passenger "Cúl an tSúdaire!"
The passenger stood up, lifted down a case from the rack,
Walked out of the coach, but did not get off the train.
For the remainder of the journey, we sat alone,
The axe and I,
All the green fields running away from us,
All our daughters grown up and gone away.

261

A Cold Wind Blew in from Lake Geneva

Belovèd daughters, I would like to be cremated
Early in the afternoon, 3.30 p.m. at the latest;
A woman to say Psalm 23;
A painter to say a poem from memory;
A poet to hold up a painting;
An architect to improvise a slow air.

Throw a party —
The kind of party that Michael Cullen
Threw in Brighton Vale in April '92,
Or in Henrietta Street in April '90:
A stand-up feast, a round table piled,
Bread and wine, the best of cheeses,
Homemade paté, olives, cucumbers,
Salami, hams, salads,
Strawberries, pineapples, melons, cream,
Bouquets of irises, daffodils, chrysanthemums,
The window open to the street.
Open all windows, let breezes
Catch napes, necks, breasts,
Cheekbones, earlobes, curtains.
When the poet Rilke died
Someone at that instant opened the bedroom window
And a cold wind blew in from Lake Geneva.

Invite by advertisement,
By word of mouth,
Anyone who felt the slightest
Affection for the deceased.

In my name drink a toast
To Human Nature and Frailty.
Whisper my two logos: Provincials To The Wall
And — Never Conform.

Later, when it suits —
When you have a weekend to spare —
Take back my ashes to Mayo,
Climb the Reek on a blue day,
Scatter my ashes in the direction of Clew Bay.
Not to worry if a west wind
Blows them back in the opposite direction —
That would be in the nature of things.

If all that is asking too much
Take my ashes out for a walk in Ringsend
Down the Drain;
No more seductive entrance to the world
Than the Drain in Ringsend;
Not even the Champs-Elysées
Quite match the Drain;
Down Pigeon House Road,
Past the Tech,
Past the Toll Bridge,
Down to the Gut;
No more seductive exit from the world
Than the Gut in Ringsend;
Not even the Statue of Liberty
Quite matches the Gut.

Cast me out into the Gut
So that one will never know exactly
Whether my ashes fetched up
In Dodder or Liffey or Grand Canal:

The thing in the end being The Mixture.
PS
If you would rather not,
I mean if all of this strikes you as too, too much,
Put my ashes in a black refuse sack and remember
To put it out on Wednesday morning
Along with the dustbin and the empties —
The golden, golden empties.

A Snail in My Prime

Slug love:
Older than the pyramids
Christ Jesus
I am a snail in my prime.

On the banks of the Boyne on a June night,
I repose under the snail cairn of Newgrange
Watching men go to the moon
While their women give birth to more women.
My snail soul is light-sensitive.
I repose in the central chamber of the passage grave
Inhaling the stillness of the earth
While my daughter daubs slime on my face,
Inserts slime in every crevice of my body,
Between my toes, behind my ears.
Small, plump, sleek thrush on wall-top with snail in beak
Banging it, cracking me open.
Between each embalming, she goes down to the river;
Returns with her hands glistening with snails.
(Oh to hold in my hands my father's walking stick
And to press to my lips its brass ferrule and to lean
On it with his chamois gloves on the handle and to test
The floor with its point—that is the point!)
I have never seen my daughter so congenial
As this evening at the signal of my burial.
I have never heard such laughter on her lips,
Such actual, gratuitous, carefree laughter.
She cries: "Thank you for bringing me to the water."
Under the corbelled roof of her own shell;

In the central chamber of her soul;
In the passage of her root;
At the entrance stone of her eyes;
Behind the kerb stones of her knees;
In the quartz stones of her ears;
In the basin stones of her elbows;
Inside the stone circle of her hair
I listen to her voice echoing in mud millennia:
"Thank you for bringing me to the water."

I like to spend Christmas in Newgrange
Alone with my extended family
In shells all of different stripes and hues
But unisoned in a bequeathal of slime.
At dawn, at the midwinter solstice,
We creep into the corbelled vault
Of the family tomb.
Down in dark
Death is a revealing of light
When a snail inherits the sky,
Inherits his own wavy lines;
When a snail comes full circle
Into the completion of his partial self.
At my life's end, I writhe
For the sun to fatten in the east
And make love to me;
To enter me
At 8.58 a.m.
And to stay inside me
For seventeen minutes,
My eyes out on stalks.
You feel like a spiral
Inside me; you feel
Like three spirals inside me.

After such early morning lovemaking –
I always preferred making love at daybreak –
I spin out my fate
Under my lady's capstone.
The snails of her breasts
Peep out from behind
Their pink petals.
At my life's end in Newgrange
There is light at the end of the tunnel.

Round and round I trundle my bundle of ego,
My nostril tumbril,
My ham pram, my heart cart,
My dreaming shell, my conscious horns,
My spiral of tongue
Unspiralling over the years,
My crops of teeth.
I am a smudge of froth. All I can hear
Is the tiny squeaking in prehistoric forests
Of my antennae being bent until they snap;
The Great Irish Snail in his prime
Coating the cones of Scots pines with his slime,
The orange aura of desire.
I am not a womanizer,
I am a snail.
When it is all over
And my daughters have eaten me,
Cremated me
In earthenware pots
With my stone beads
And there will be from me no more poems,
No more antler, no more horn,
And the last tourist coaches have departed,
Morsels of my antennae will be plucked up

By departing house martins, digested,
Deposited off the shores of Africa
In plankton of the South Seas
To enter into the bloodstream of sea lions . . .
Last night, when we made love up behind our pillows,
A pair of sea lions mated on a sud-strewn rock,
Who moments ago were snails in separate beds,
The River Boyne curled up at our feet,
My tail in your tail, my slime in your slime.

Slug love:
Older than the pyramids
Christ Jesus
I am a snail in my prime.

GLOSSARY